To Mother
David
7/15/75.

A CONCISE
TREASURY OF
BIBLE QUOTATIONS

A
CONCISE
TREASURY
OF
BIBLE
QUOTATIONS

by
Robert Garvey

jD | JONATHAN DAVID PUBLISHERS, INC.
MIDDLE VILLAGE, N.Y. 11379

A CONCISE TREASURY OF BIBLE QUOTATIONS
by
ROBERT GARVEY
Copyright © 1975
by
JONATHAN DAVID PUBLISHERS, INC.
MIDDLE VILLAGE, N.Y. 11379

Library of Congress Cataloging in Publication Data

Bible. English. Selections. 1974.
A concise treasury of Bible quotations.

I. Garvey, Robert, ed. II. Title.
BS391.2.037   220.5'2   74-1966
ISBN 0-8246-0184-9

FOREWORD

A Concise Treasury of Bible Quotations provides the modern reader with a rich sampling of the greatest thoughts, phrases, and other writings of both the "Old" and "New" Testaments of the Bible, arranged alphabetically by topic for easy reference.

In this volume, the professional — the writer, teacher and student of religion, the minister, priest and rabbi — has instant access (with source given in chapter and verse) to what the Bible has to say about God, Love, Good and Evil, Kindness, Equal Justice Under the Law, Child and Parent Relationships, Labor and Business Practices, War and Peace, Ecology, Women, and other subjects on the minds of all thinking people today.

This concise treasury contains portions of such memorable psalms as the beloved 23rd (complete); the 90th ("Lord, You have been our dwelling-place in all generations"); the 104th, in praise of God the Creator; the 139th ("O Lord, You have looked into me, and You know me"); the 91st and 46th, about God the Protector ("He is my refuge and my fortress" and "A very present help in trouble"); and the 100th, a psalm of thanksgiving ("Shout joyfully to the Lord, all you lands!")

Also, generous portions of the most beautiful hymns and prayers, parables and prophecies in the Bible: "The Song of Moses," the perfect lyric poem extolling God for His faithfulness to His people; "Deborah's Song of Triumph," earliest Hebrew literary masterpiece (composed about 1125 BCE); "The Song of Hannah," lyric on the dedication of her son Samuel, foreshadowing Mary's hymn of gratitude, "The Magnificat" (also here); the "Benedictus" of Zacharias, after his aged wife gave birth to John (the Baptist); Jesus' parables, "The Lost Sheep," "The Prodigal Son," etc.; "The Sermon on the Mount," including "The Beatitudes," "The Lord's Prayer," and "The Golden Rule"; Isaiah's vision of universal peace ("And they shall beat their swords into plowshares"); and other magnificent writings.

You don't have to be Jewish, Christian, or anything else, to profit from these sparkling gems of wisdom and insight, the heritage of all Western civilization. As a layman, you can peruse the pages of this treasury for religious instruction, for inspiration, or simply for the joy of meeting new and old literary friends; as a professional you will find it useful as a tool of reference.

A word about the language: in general we have used the King James Version, that most majestic of English translations. But since Scripture is more than beauty of speech, to make the meaning clear for today's reader we have taken the liberty of updating certain archaic words and phrases.

Finally, my warm thanks to my wife Miriam for her help.

ROBERT GARVEY

A CONCISE TREASURY
OF BIBLE QUOTATIONS

ACTION

Faith Without Action

Faith, if it has not works, is dead ... Show me your faith without your works, and I will show you my faith by my works ... Was not Abraham our father justified by works, when he had offered Isaac his son upon the altar? As the body without the spirit is dead, so faith without works is dead also.

James 2: 15-26

Words Without Action

If a brother or sister are without clothes and without food for the day, and you say to them, "Go in peace, be warmed and well fed," without giving them those things needed for the body, what help is that?

James 2:15

ADULTERY

David Covets Bath-sheba

One evening, David rose from his couch and walked out upon the roof of the palace. From there, he saw a woman bathing, a very beautiful woman. David asked who she was and someone said:

"Isn't it Bath-sheba, the wife of Uriah the Hittite?" David sent for her and lay with her.

2 Samuel 11:2-4

God's Commandment

You shall not commit adultery.

Exodus 20:13

Lustful Looking

Whoever looks at a woman to lust after her has committed adultery with her already in his heart.

Matthew 5:28

7

Walking on Coals

Can a man take fire in his bosom
And his clothes not be burned?
Can one walk on hot coals
And his feet not be burned?
So he who goes in to his neighbor's wife:
Whoever touches her shall not be innocent.

Proverbs 6:27-29

AGE

On Youth

Rejoice, O young man, in your youth
And let your heart be glad in the days of your youth.
And walk in the ways of your heart . . .

Ecclesiastes 11:9

On Old Age

Remember your Creator in the days of your youth,
Before the evil days come
And the years draw near when you will say,
"I have no pleasure in them" . . .
Before the silver cord is snapped . . .
And the dust returns to the earth as it was,
And the spirit returns to God who gave it.

Ecclesiastes 11;12:1, 6-8

How to Reprove

Rebuke not an elder, but intreat him as a father; and the younger men as brethren; the elder women as mothers; the younger as sisters, with all purity.

1 Timothy 5:1-2

Bearing the Yoke

It is good for a man that he bear the yoke in his youth.

Lamentations 3:27

ANGER

Slow to Anger

Let every man be swift to hear, slow to speak, slow to anger.

James 1:19

Ruling One's Temper

He who is slow to anger is better than the mighty; And he who rules his temper, than he who conquers a city.

Proverbs 16:32

The Sensible Man

It is sensible for a man to be slow to anger; It is his glory to pass over a transgression.

Proverbs 19:1

Harboring Anger

Let not the sun go down upon your wrath.

Ephesians 4:26

APPEARANCE

Man vs. the Lord

Man looks on the outward appearance, but the Lord looks into the heart.

1 Samuel 16:7

Do Not Judge

Judge not according to the appearance.

John 7:24

Solomon's Prayer

"You, You only, know what is in the hearts of all the children of men."

1 Kings 8:39

ARK

Moses Prays in the Desert

When the ark was carried forward, Moses said:
"Rise up, O Lord! Let Your enemies be scattered;
and let those who hate You flee before You."

And when it was brought to rest, he said:
"Return, O Lord, to the ten thousands of the families of
Israel "

Numbers 10:35-36

King David Brings the
Ark to Jerusalem

Lift up your heads, O gates,
That the King of glory may come in!

"Who is the King of glory?
The Lord strong and mighty,
The Lord mighty in battle."
Lift up your heads, O gates,
Yes, lift them up, everlasting doors,
That the King of glory may come in!
"Who is the King of glory?
The Lord of hosts:
He is the King of glory."

Psalms 24:7-10

The Taking of Jericho

On the seventh day, they rose at dawn and marched around the city with the ark of the Lord seven times. And at the seventh time, when the priests blew with their horns, Joshua said to the people: "Shout! — for the Lord has given you the city!"

Joshua 6:15-16

BIRTH

The Birth of Isaac

God said to Abraham:
"As for Sarai your wife, you shall not call her Sarai, but Sarah (Princess) shall be her name. I will give you a son of her and you shall call him Isaac; I will bless her, and she shall be a mother of nations; kings of peoples shall be descended from her."
Then Abraham fell upon his face, and laughed, and said in his heart: "Shall a child be born to a man who is a hundred years old? Shall Sarah, who is ninety, give birth?"

Genesis 17:15-17

* * *

And Sarah conceived and bore Abraham a son, whom Abraham called Isaac . . . And Sarah said: "God has made laughter for me; and every one who hears will laugh on account of me. Who would have said to Abraham that Sarah would be nursing a child—having borne him a son in his old age!"

Genesis 21:1-7

The Birth of Samson

There was a certain man, Manoah, whose wife was barren. And the angel of the Lord appeared to the woman, and said:

"Drink no wine nor strong drink, and eat no unclean thing. For, lo, you shall conceive and bear a son. And no razor is to come upon his head, for the child shall be a Nazirite to God from birth; and he shall begin to save Israel out of the hand of the Philistines."

. . . And the woman bore a son, and called him Samson. And the child grew, and the Lord blessed him.

Judges 13:2-5, 24

The Birth of Samuel

Hannah prayed to the Lord and vowed:

"O Lord of Hosts, if you will indeed look on my affliction and not forget your handmaid but will give me a manchild, then I will give him to the Lord all the days of his life, and no razor shall come upon his head."

So Hannah conceived and bore a son, whom she called Samuel, "because I have asked him of the Lord."

1 Samuel 1:11, 20

Elisha and the Shunamite

Elisha sent for the barren Shunamite, who had treated him and his servant with kindness, and he told her:

"At this time next year you shall be holding a baby son."

"Oh, no, my Lord!" she said, since her husband was on in years. "Do not mislead your handmaid!"

But the woman did conceive, and bore a baby son by the same time next year, as Elisha had told her.

2 Kings 4:14-17

The Birth of John the Baptist

And the angel said to the priest Zacharias:

"Don't be afraid. Your prayer has been heard, and your wife Elisabeth shall bear you a son and you shall call him John. And many shall rejoice at his birth. He shall be great in the sight of the Lord, and shall drink neither wine nor strong drink and he shall be filled with the Holy Spirit from birth. And many of the children of Israel shall he turn to the Lord their God."

Zacharias said: "How can I know this is so? For I am an old man and my wife is advanced in years."

The angel answered: "I am Gabriel. I stand in the presence of God who sent me to speak to you, and to bring you this good news."

. . . And his wife Elisabeth conceived. And she said: "Now at last the Lord has taken away my public humiliation."

Luke 1:13-19, 24

The Birth of Jesus

Now the angel Gabriel was sent from God to a town in Galilee called Nazareth, to a girl betrothed to a man named Joseph who was descended from King David, and the girl's name was Mary.

And the angel said:

"Blessed are you among women! Don't be afraid, Mary, for you have found grace with God. You will conceive and give birth to a son and you shall call him Jesus. He shall be great and shall be called the Son of the Most High. The Lord will give him the throne of his father, David: and he shall reign over the descendents of Jacob forever; and of his kingdom there shall be no end."

Mary said, "But I am a virgin. How will this happen?"

The angel answered:

"The Holy Spirit will come on you and God's power will rest on you. Therefore your holy child will be called the Son of God. Look at your cousin Elisabeth. Although she has always been barren, she has conceived a son in her old age and is now in her sixth month. Nothing is impossible with God."

And Mary said:

"I am the handmaid of the Lord. Let it be as you say."

Luke 1:26-37

The Benedictus of Zacharias

And Zacharias, responding to his neighbors' wonder about his new-born child, John, prophesied, saying:

"Blessed be the Lord God of Israel; for He has visited and redeemed His people,

"And has raised up a horn of salvation for us in the house of His servant David;

"As He spoke by the mouth of His holy ones, the prophets of old;

"That we should be saved from our enemies, and from the hand of all that hate us;

"To perform the mercy promised to our fathers, and to remember His holy covenant;

"The oath which He swore to our father Abraham,

"That He would grant unto us, that, delivered out of the hand of our enemies, we might serve Him without fear,

"In holiness and righteousness before Him, all the days.

"And you, child, shall be called the prophet of the Most High: for you shall go before the face of the Lord to prepare His ways,

"To give to his people knowledge of salvation through forgiveness of their sins,

"Through the tender mercy of our God; whereby the bright dawn from on high has visited us,

"To give light to those who sit in darkness and in the shadow of death, to guide our feet into the way of peace."

And the child grew, and waxed strong in body and spirit, and was in the desert till the day of his appearing to the people of Israel.

Luke 1:68-80

BOASTING

Self-Praise

Let another praise you, and not your own mouth; A stranger, and not your own lips.

Proverbs 27:2

Talk Not Proud

Talk no more so exceedingly proud; let not arrogancy come out of your mouth: for the Lord is a God of knowledge, and by Him actions are weighed.

1 Samuel 2:3

Time Brings Changes

Do not boast of tomorrow, for you never know what a day brings forth.

Proverbs 27:1

The Bribe Blinds

You shall take no bribe: for the bribe blinds the wise, and perverts the words of the righteous.

Exodus 23:8

Sinners and Bloody Men

Gather not my soul with sinners,
Nor my life with bloody men:
In whose hands is mischief,
And their right hand is full of bribes.

Psalms 26:9-10

BROTHERS

Joseph Reveals His Identity

Unable to restrain himself before his attendants, Joseph sent them out of the chamber and he made himself known to his brothers. Weeping aloud, he said to them:
"I am Joseph! Is my father still alive and well?"
His brothers, astounded, could not answer him.
"Come closer to me," Joseph said. And he continued: "I am Joseph, your brother, whom you sold into Egypt! And now be not grieved, nor angry with yourselves that you sold me here; for God sent me before you to save lives. It was not you sent me here, but God . . . God has made me a father to Pharaoh, lord of all his household, and ruler over all the land of Egypt."

Genesis 45:5-9

The Hands of Esau

Jacob went near Isaac, his father, who felt him and said:
"The voice is the voice of Jacob, but the hands are the hands of Esau."

Genesis 27:22

BROTHERHOOD

The Common Bond

The rich and the poor meet together — The Lord is the maker of them all.

Proverbs 22:2

Mankind as Brothers

"Are you not as the children of the Ethiopians to Me, O children of Israel?" says the Lord.

Amos 9:7

Children of God

For you are all the children of God by faith in Christ Jesus. . . . There is neither Jew nor Greek, slave nor freeman, male nor female: for you are all one in Christ Jesus.

Galatians 3:26-28

Living Brotherhood

Behold, how good and how pleasant it is for brethren to dwell together in unity!

Psalms 133:1

Abraham Settles a Quarrel

Abraham said to Lot:
"Let there be no strife between you and me, or between your herdsmen and mine, for we are kinsmen. Is not the whole land before you? Let us separate. If you want to go to the left, I will go to the right; if you prefer the right, I will go to the left."

Genesis 13:8-9

Loving Your Brother

If anyone says, "I love God," and hates his brother, he is a liar; for he who does not love his brother whom he has seen, cannot love God whom he has not seen.

1 John 4:20

If anyone has the world's goods and sees his brother in need, yet closes his heart against him, how does God's love abide in him?

1 John 3:17

* * *

And Jonathan caused David to swear again for the love that he had for him; for he loved him as he loved his own soul.

1 Samuel 20:17

* * *

You shall not hate your brother in your heart; you shall surely rebuke your neighbor.

Leviticus 19:17

* * *

If your brother shall trespass against you, go and tell him his fault between you and him alone: if he shall hear you, you have gained your brother.

Matthew 18:15

* * *

If your enemy be hungry, give him bread to eat, And if he be thirsty, give him water to drink.

Proverbs 25:21

CHARITY

In Praise of Charity

Though I speak with the tongues of men and of angels, and have not charity, I am become as sounding brass, or a tinkling cymbal. Though I have the gift of prophecy and understand all mysteries and all knowledge; and though I have the faith to move mountains, and have not charity, I am nothing. Though I bestow all my goods to feed the poor, and though I give my body to be burned, and have not charity, it profits me nothing.

Charity is patient and kind· charity envies not; charity does not vaunt itself, is not puffed up.

1 Corinthians 13:1-4

The Virtues of Charity

Charity bears all things, believes all things, hopes all things, endures all things.

Charity never fails.

1 Corinthians 13:7-8

The Greatest Virtue

Now abides faith, hope, charity; but the greatest of these is charity.

Corinthians 13:13

Peter Extols Charity

Charity covers a multitude of sins.

1 Peter 4:8

CHASTITY

Lust Not

Lust not after her beauty in your heart; Neither let her take you with her eyelids.

Proverbs 6:25

CHEERFULNESS

A Continual Feast

He who is of a merry heart has a continual feast.

Proverbs 15:15

CHILDREN

In Praise of Children

As arrows are in the hand of a mighty man,
So are the children of one's youth.
Happy is the man who has his quiver full of them.

Psalms 127:4-5

The Glory of the Young

Children's children are the crown of old men; And the glory of children are their fathers.

Proverbs 17:6

The Lord's Heritage

Lo, children are a heritage of the Lord: And the fruit of the womb is a reward.

Psalms 127:3

Heaven's Welcome

Except that you be converted and become as little children, you shall not enter the kingdom of heaven.

Matthew 18:3

Babes and Sucklings

Out of the mouth of babes and sucklings you have perfected praise.

Matthew 21:16

Bringing Up Children

Train up a child in the way he should go, And even when he is old, he will not depart from it.

Proverbs 22:6

Teaching a Child

The rod and reproof give wisdom; But a child left to himself causes shame to his mother.

Proverbs 29:15

The Soul's Delight

Correct your son, and he will give you rest; Yes, he will give delight to your soul.

Proverbs 29:17

Loving a Son

He who spares his rod hates his son; But he who loves him chastens him betimes.

Proverbs 13:24

Punishing with Restraint

Chasten your son, for there is hope; But set not your heart on his destruction.

Proverbs 19:18

A Father's Duty

The father to the children shall make known Your truth.

Isaiah 38:19

Responsibilities of Children

Honor your father and your mother, as the Lord your God commanded you; that your days may be long, and that it may go well with you, upon the land which the Lord your God has given you.

Deuteronomy 5:16

A Wreath of Grace

Hear, my son, the instruction of your father,
And forsake not the teaching of your mother;
For they shall be a wreath of grace to your head,
And necklaces about your neck.

Proverbs 1:8-9

The Wise Son

A wise son is instructed by his father; But a scorner hears not rebuke.

Proverbs 13:1

The Foolish Son

A foolish son is vexation to his father, And bitterness to her who bore him.

Proverbs 18:25

CHOICES

Choose Between God and Baal!

Elijah came near the people and said:
"How long will you halt between two opinions? If the Lord be God, follow Him; but if Baal, follow him."

1 Kings 18:21

Choose Life

I have set before you life and death, the blessing and the curse; therefore choose life, that you may live.

Deuteronomy 30:19

Who to Serve?

Choose you this day whom you will serve.

Joshua 24:15

CHURCH

The Church on the Rock

You are Peter, and upon this rock I will build my church: and the gates of hell shall not prevail against it. I will give to you the keys of the kingdom of heaven and whatever you shall bind on earth shall be bound in heaven; and whatever you shall loose on earth shall be loosed in heaven.

Matthew 16:18-19

Qualifications of a Bishop

If a man desire the office of a bishop, he desires a good work.
A bishop then must be blameless, the husband of one wife, vigilant, sober, of good behavior, hospitable, a good teacher,

not given to wine, not greedy of filthy lucre: but patient, not a brawler, not covetous. (For if a man know not how to rule his own house, how shall he take care of the church of God?) Not a novice, lest being lifted up with pride he fall into the condemnation of the devil. Moreover, he must have a good report of those outside the church, lest he fall into reproach and the snare of the devil.

1 Timothy 3:1-7

A Patient Teacher

The servant of the Lord must not be quarrelsome; but be gentle to all men, a good and patient teacher, gently correcting.

2 Timothy 2:24

COMMANDMENTS

The Ten Commandments

Then God spoke all these words:
I am the Lord your God, who brought you out of the land of Egypt, out of the house of bondage.
You shall have no other gods before Me . . .
You shall not take the name of the Lord your God in vain . . .
Remember the Sabbath day, to keep it holy.
Honor your father and your mother.
You shall not murder.
You shall not commit adultery.
You shall not steal.
You shall not bear false witness.
You shall not covet.

Exodus 20:1-14

Not Beyond Reach

This commandment which I command you this day [to keep God's commandments], it is not too hard for you, neither is it far off. It is not in heaven, that you should say: "Who shall go up for us to heaven, and bring it unto us, and make us hear it, that we may do it?" Neither is it beyond the sea, that you should say: "Who shall go over the sea for us, and bring it to us and make us hear it, that we may do it?" But the word is very near to you, in your mouth and in your heart, that you may do it.

Deuteronomy 30:11-14

The Choice is Yours

See, I have set before you this day life and good, death and evil, in that I command you this day to love the Lord your God, to walk in His ways, and to keep His commandments; then you shall live and multiply, and the Lord your God shall bless you in the land whither you go in to possess it. But if your heart turn away, and you will not hear . . . you shall not prolong your days upon the land . . . I have set before you life and death, the blessing and the curse. Therefore choose life.

Deuteronomy 30:15-19

Keep the Commandments

And now, Israel, what does the Lord your God require of you, but to fear the Lord your God, to walk in all His ways, and to love Him, and to serve the Lord your God with all your heart and with all your soul; to keep for your good the commandments of the Lord, and His statutes. Therefore you shall love the Lord your God, and keep His commandments, always.

Deuteronomy 10:11-13; 11

* * *

The end of the matter, all having been heard: fear God, and keep His commandments; for this is the whole man.

Ecclesiastes 12:13

The Greatness of God's Law

The law of the Lord is perfect, restoring the soul;
The testimony of the Lord is sure, making wise the sim-
ple.
The precepts of the Lord are right, rejoicing the heart;
The commandment of the Lord is pure, enlightening the
eyes.
The fear of the Lord is clean, enduring forever;
The ordinances of the Lord are true, and righteous al-
together;
More to be desired are they than gold, yes, than much
fine gold;
Sweeter also than honey and the honeycomb . . .

Psalms 19:8-11

* * *

Your word is a lamp to my feet,
And a light to my path.

Psalms 119:105

A Reminder

The Lord spoke to Moses saying: "Tell the children of Israel to make fringes in the corners of their garments, with the fringe of each corner a thread of blue, to look upon it and remember to do all My commandments."

Numbers 15:37-40

The Greatest

Someone asked him:
"Master, which is the great commandment of the law?"
Jesus said:
"You shall love the Lord your God with all your heart, and with all your soul, and with all your mind. This the first and great commandment. And the second is like it: You shall love your neighbor as yourself. On these two commandments hang all the law and the prophets."

Matthew 22:35-40

Man's Duty

Fear God, and keep His commandments: for this is the whole duty of man.

Ecclesiastes 12:13

Road to Eternal Life

Someone said to Jesus: "Good Master, what good thing shall I do, that I may have eternal life?"
"Why call me good?" he answered. "There is none good but one, and that is God; but if you will enter into life, keep the commandments."
"Which commandments?"
"You shall do no murder. You shall not commit adultery. You shall not steal. You shall not bear false witness. Honor your father and your mother; and you shall love your neighbor as yourself."

Matthew 19:16-19

The Law

Think not that I have come to destroy the law, or the prophets: I have not come to destroy but to fulfill.

Matthew 5:17

* * *

It is easier for heaven and earth to pass than one tittle of the law to fail.

Luke 16:17

Fulfilling the Law

He who loves another has fulfilled the law.

Romans 13:8

Troubler of Israel

When King Ahab saw Elijah, he said:
"Is it you, you troubler of Israel?"
Elijah answered: "I have not troubled Israel; but you, and your father's house, in that you have forsaken the commandments of the Lord, and have followed the Baalim!"

1 Kings 18:17

COMPASSION

Respecting Animals

If a bird's nest chance to be before you in the way, in any tree or on the ground, with young ones or eggs, and the dam sitting upon the young, or upon the eggs, you shall not take the dam with the young; you shall in any wise let the dam go, although you may take the young.

Deuteronomy 22:6-7

Compassion for the Ox

You shall not muzzle the ox when he treads out the corn.

Deuteronomy 25:4

Your Neighbor's Property

You shall not see your neighbor's ox or his sheep driven away, and ignore them; you shall surely bring them back. If your neighbor does not live near you, and you do not know him, then you shall bring it home to your house, and keep it with you until he requires it, then you shall restore it to him. So you shall do likewise with his ass, his garment, or anything which he has lost and you have found; you may not be unconcerned.

You shall not see your neighbor's ass or his ox fallen down on the road and pass by; you must help him lift it up again.

Deuteronomy 22:1-4

The Golden Rule

As you would that men should do to you, do also to them.

Luke 6:31

*   *   *

All things whatever you would that men should do to you, do so to them: for this is the law and the prophets.

Matthew 7:12

Micah's Teachings

Render true judgment, and show mercy and compassion toward each other; do not oppress the widow or the fatherless, the stranger, or the poor...

Zechariah 7:8-10

The Strong and the Weak

We who are strong ought to bear the infirmities of the weak.

Romans 15:1

CONFESSION

The Road to Mercy

He who covers up his sins shall not prosper; But whoever confesses and forsakes them shall have mercy.

Proverbs 28:13

Earning Forgiveness

Happy is he whose transgression is forgiven, whose sin
is pardoned . . . .
When I kept silence, my bones wore away
Through groaning all day long.
For day and night Your hand was heavy upon me . . . .
I said: "I will make confession concerning my transgres-
sion to the Lord" —
And You forgave the guilt of my sin.

Psalms 32:1, 3, 5

COURAGE

Be Strong

Be strong and of a good courage; be not afraid, neither be thou dismayed. The Lord thy God is with thee wherever thou goest.

Joshua 1:9

Courage of the Heart

Be strong, and let your heart take courage, All you who wait for the Lord.

Psalms 31:25

Man's Helper

The Lord is my helper, and I will not fear what man shall do to me.

Hebrews 13:6

David and Goliath

King Saul dressed David in his own fighting gear, with his helmet of brass on his head, his coat of mail and his own sword. But David was scarcely able to move about; he had never worn armor before. So he said to Saul:

"I cannot wear these, because I have never tried them." And he took them off. He took his staff in hand, chose five smooth stones from the brook and put them in his shepherd's bag. With his sling in hand, he drew near to the Philistine.

1 Samuel 17:38-40

COVENANT

God's Promise

The Lord said to Abram:

"Get you out of your country, and from your kindred, and from your father's house, to the land that I will show you. I will make of you a great nation and I will bless you. I will make your name great, and it shall be a blessing. I will bless those who bless you, and curse those who curse you; and in you shall all the families of the earth be blessed.

Genesis 12:1-3

A Father of Nations

When Abram was ninety-nine years old, the Lord appeared to him and said:

"I . . . will establish My covenant with you to be your God and the God of your descendants. And I will give you and your descendants the land where you sojourn, the whole land of Canaan, for an everlasting possession. Your name shall no longer be Abram, but Abraham; for the father of a multitude of nations have I made you. And this is the mark of My covenant which you shall keep between Me and you and your descendants: every male among you shall be circumcised when he is eight days old. . . . As for your wife, you shall not call her Sarai but Sarah. I will bless her . . . and she shall become a mother of nations, and kings of peoples shall stem from her."

Genesis 17:1-16

A Holy Nation

You shall be to me a kingdom of priests and a holy nation.

Exodus 19:6

The People Promise

Joshua said:

"Thus says the Lord: 'I gave you a land on which you had not labored, and cities to dwell in which you had not built; and you eat from vineyards and olive-groves which you never planted. Now choose whether you will serve the Lord or alien gods.' "

The people cried: "We will serve the Lord!"

So Joshua made a covenant with the people that day and wrote these words in the book of the Law of God; and he set a great stone under the oak that was by the sanctuary of the Lord. And he said: "Behold, this stone shall be a witness."

Joshua 24:1, 13-18, 20-28

The Israelites Accept

Moses came and told the people all the commands and ordinances of the Lord; and all the people answered with one voice:

"All the commands which the Lord has spoken we shall do!"

Exodus 24:3

Your Own Witnesses

Joshua said to the people:
"You are your own witnesses that you have chosen to serve the Lord." And they replied, "We are witnesses."

Joshua 24:22

Remember the Covenant

For the mountains may depart and the hills be removed, but My concern shall not depart from you.

Isaiah 54:10

God's Pledge

And I will betroth you to Me forever. I will betroth you to Me in righteousness and in justice . . . and you shall know the Lord.

Hosea 2:21-22

The Burden of the Chosen

"You only have I known of all the families of the earth; Therefore will I punish you for all your iniquities."

Amos 3:2

The Israelites
Reaffirm Allegiance to God

On the first day of the seventh month, the people gathered as one man in the broad place before the water gate and they called Ezra the scribe to bring out the book of the Law of Moses which the Lord had commanded Israel.

So Ezra brought the Law before the congregation of men, women and all children old enough to understand. Standing on a raised wooden platform that had been made for the purpose, he read out of the book from dawn to midday while the Levites explained the Law. As the people listened attentively, they wept at the words. Then Nehemiah, who was the governor, and Ezra, the priest and scribe, and the Levites who taught the people, said to the people:

"Do not weep or be sad! This day is holy to the Lord your God. Rejoice!"

Ezra then opened the scroll so that all could see it, and as he opened it, all the people stood up. Ezra blessed the Lord, the great God, and all the people, with their hands lifted high, answered: "Amen, Amen!" Then they bowed their heads and prostrated themselves before the Lord with their faces to the ground.

Nehemiah 8

CREATION

In the Beginning

In the beginning God created the heaven and the earth . . .

God said: "Let there be light," and there was light. God saw that the light was good and He separated the light from the darkness . . . There was evening and there was morning, one day.

Then God said: "Let there be a firmament dividing the waters under the firmament from the waters above the firmament," and God called the firmament, *heaven.* And there was evening and morning, a second day.

Then God said: "Let the waters under the heaven be gathered to one place, so the dry land can appear." It was so. God called the dry land, *the earth*, and the gathering of the waters, *the sea.* God saw that it was good.

Then God said: "Let the earth bring forth grass, plants yielding seed, and all kinds of fruit trees yielding fruit, with its seed in it . . . "God saw that it was good. And there was evening and morning, a third day.

God said: "Let there be lights in the heavens to separate day from night; and let them mark the seasons, and the days and years; and let them be for lights in the heaven to give light upon the earth." It was so. God made the two great lights, the greater light to rule the day, and the lesser light to rule the night; and He made the stars. God set them in the heaven to give light upon the earth . . . and to separate the light from the darkness. God saw that it was good. And there was evening and morning, a fourth day.

God said: "Let the waters swarm with living creatures, and let birds fly above the earth under the heavens." And so it was.

God created the great sea monsters and every swimming creature with which the waters swarm, and every kind of winged bird. God saw that it was good, and He blessed them, saying:

"Be fruitful and multiply, and fill the waters of the seas; and let the birds multiply on the earth." There was evening and morning, a fifth day.

Then God said: "Let the earth bring forth all kinds of living creatures, cattle, reptiles and wild beasts." God saw that it was good.

Then God said: "Let us make man in our image, after our likeness; and let them have dominion over the fish in the sea, over the birds of the air, over the cattle, and the animals of the earth, and over every creeping thing upon the earth."

God created man in His own image, in the image of God He created him; male and female, He created them.

Then God blessed them, saying:

"Be fruitful and multiply; fill the earth and subdue it. Have mastery over the fish of the sea, the birds of the air, and every living thing that creeps on the earth."

God said: "See, I give you every plant of the earth yielding seed, and every tree with seed-bearing fruit for your food. To every beast of the earth, every bird of the air, and to everything that creeps on the earth, I give all the green plants for food." And it was so.

God saw everything that He had made, and it was very good. There was evening and there was morning, the sixth day.

Since on the seventh day God was finished with the work of creation, He rested on the seventh day from His work. And God blessed the seventh day and made it holy.

Genesis 1, 2:1-3

How Man Was Created

The Lord God formed man of the dust of the ground, and breathed into his nostrils the breath of life; and man became a living being.

Genesis 2:7

How Woman Was Created

The Lord God said: "It is not good that the man should be alone; I will make him a partner." So the Lord God caused a deep sleep to fall on the man, and while he slept, He took one of his ribs and closed up the place with flesh. And from the rib, which the Lord God had taken from the man, He made a woman. When He brought her to the man, the man said: "This is now bone of my bones, and flesh of my flesh; she shall be called Woman, because she was taken out of Man."

Therefore does a man leave his father and mother, and

cleave to his wife, and they become as one flesh.

Genesis 2:18-24

In God's Image

So God created man in His own image, in the image of God created He him, male and female.

Genesis 1:27

God, the Maker

What is man that You are mindful of him? You have made him a little lower than the angels.

Psalms 8:4, 5

* * *

I am fearfully and wonderfully made.

Psalms 139:14

* * *

We are the clay and You, O Lord, our potter.

Isaiah 64:8

* * *

The Lord God formed man of the dust of the ground, and breathed into his nostrils the breath of life; and man became a living soul.

Genesis 2:7

* * *

And from the rib, which the Lord God had taken from the man, God made a woman, and brought her to the man.

Genesis 2:22

DEATH

Loss of a Leader

After the death of Moses, God spoke to Joshua:
"Be strong and of good courage ... to observe and do according to all the laws which Moses, My servant, commanded you."

Joshua 1:6-7

David's Advice

Now the days of David drew near that he should die and he charged Solomon his son, saying, "I go the way of all the earth;

be strong therefore and show yourself a man, and keep the charge of the Lord your God to walk in His ways . . ."

1 Kings 2:1-3

Man's Inescapable Fate

Isaiah came to Hezekiah and said to him:
"Thus says the Lord; set your house in order for you shall die and not live."

2 Kings 20:1

The Death of Death

He will swallow up death forever, and the Lord God will wipe away tears from off all faces.

Isaiah 25:8

To Everything a Season

There is a time to be born, and a time to die.

Ecclesiastes 3:2

Man, the Mortal

Man is like a breath; his days are as a shadow that passes away.

Psalms 144:3-4

* * *

We must die, and are as water spilt on the ground, which cannot be gathered up again.

2 Samuel 14:14

* * *

As for man, his days are as grass: as a flower of the field, so he flourishes.

Psalms 103:15

* * *

Shall mortal man be just before God?

Job 4:17

As a Tale Ends

We bring our years to an end as a tale that is told.

Psalms 90:9

A Covenant

We have made a covenant with death.

Isaiah 28:15

Man's Enemy

The last enemy that shall be destroyed is death.

1 Corinthians 15:26

The Name of Death

I looked and beheld a pale horse:
And his name who sat on him was Death.

Revelation 6:8

Jesus' Glory

Jesus, who was made a little lower than the angels for the suffering of death, crowned with glory and honor; that he by the grace of God should taste death for every man.

Hebrews 2:9

A Common Fate

Man born of woman
Is of few days, and full of trouble.
He comes forth like a flower, and withers;
He flees also as a shadow, and continues not.

Job 14:1-2

O Death!

"O death, where is your victory?
O death, where is your sting?"

1 Corinthians 15:54-55

David Resumes His Life

David answered his servants:
"While my child was alive I fasted and wept . . . But now he is dead, why should I fast? Can I bring him back again? I shall go to him, but he will not return to me."

2 Samuel 12:22-23

The Lord's Will

The Lord gave and the Lord has taken away, blessed be the name of the Lord.

Job 1:21

Treasure the Living

A living dog is better than a dead lion.

Ecclesiastes 9:4

Dust to Dust

And the dust returns to the earth as it was and the spirit returns to God Who gave it.

Ecclesiastes 12:7

Swifter Than Eagles

Your beauty, O Israel, upon your high places is slain!
How are the mighty fallen!

Tell it not in Gath,
Publish it not in the streets of Ashkelon;
Lest the daughters of the heathen triumph ·

O mountains of Gilboa,
Let there be no dew nor rain upon you,
Neither fields of choice fruits;
For there the shield of the mighty was vilely cast away,
The shield of Saul, not anointed with oil . . .

Saul and Jonathan were lovely and pleasant in their
    lives,
And in their death they were not divided,
They were swifter than eagles,
They were stronger than lions!

I am distressed for you, my brother Jonathan;
Very dear have you been to me;
Your love to me was wonderful,
Passing the love of women.

How are the mighty fallen,
And the weapons of war perished!

2 Samuel 1:7-27

The Death of Moses

Moses went up from the plains of Moab to Mount Nebo, the

top of Pisgah, which faces Jericho, and the Lord showed him all the land . . .

The Lord said: "This is the land which I swore to Abraham, Isaac, and Jacob, saying I would give it to their descendants. I have let you see it with your eyes, but you shall not enter it." So Moses, the servant of the Lord, died there in the land of Moab, as the Lord had said. And he was buried in the valley of Moab over against Beth-peor; and to this day no man knows his burial place . . .

For thirty days the children of Israel wept for Moses in the plains of Moab until the time of grief and mourning were ended.

And there has not since arisen a prophet in Israel like Moses, whom the Lord knew face to face.

Deuteronomy 34:1-10

DECEIT

As a cage is full of birds, so are their houses full of deceit.

Jeremiah 5:27

God Rejects Deceit

He who works deceit shall not dwell in My house: He who tells lies shall not tarry in My sight.

Psalms 101:7

Fooling Your Neighbor

As a lunatic who scatters firebrand and arrows,
So is the man who deceives his neighbor and says, "I was only fooling."

Proverbs 26:18-19

DRUNKENNESS

The Effects of Wine

Who cries: "Woe"? Who: "Alas"?
Who has quarrels? Who has raving?
Who has redness of eyes?
Who has wounds without cause?
Those who tarry long at the wine;
Look not upon the wine when it is red,
When it glides down smoothly;

At the last it bites like a serpent,
And stings like an adder.
Your eyes shall behold strange things,
And your heart shall utter confused things.
Yes, you shall be as he who lies down in the midst of the sea,
Or as he who lies upon the top of a mast.
"They have struck me but I felt it not,
They have beaten me, but I knew it not.
When shall I awake? I will seek wine once again."

Proverbs 23:29-35

The Unwise Man

Wine is a mocker, strong drink is raging and whoever is deceived by it is not wise.

Proverbs 20:1

Sing to the Lord

Be not drunk with wine, wherein is excess; but be filled with the Spirit; speaking to yourselves in psalms and hymns and spiritual songs, singing and making melody in your heart to the Lord.

Ephasians 5:18-19

What the Lord Abhors

Woe to those who rise up early in the morning to take strong drink, who tarry late into the night till wine inflame them! The harp and the psaltery, the tabret and the pipe, and wine are in their feasts, but they regard not the work of the Lord.

Isaiah 5:11-12

ENCOURAGEMENT

Strength from God

Be strong in the Lord, and in the power of His might.

Ephasians 6:10

The Prize-Winner

Know you not that of all who run in the race, only one receives the prize? So run, that you may win.

Corinthians 9:22, 24

ENEMIES

Paying Back Evil

Do not say, "I will pay back evil."

Proverbs 20:22

Enemies and Peace

When a man's ways please the Lord, He makes even his enemies at peace with him.

Proverbs 16:7

The Enemy Falls

Do not rejoice when your enemy falls and let your heart not be glad when he stumbles.

Proverbs 24:17

Blessing the Cursed

Love your enemies, bless those who curse you, do good to those who hate you, and pray for those who persecute you.

Matthew 5:44

Helping Your Enemy

If you see your enemy's ox or his ass going astray, you shall surely bring it back to him again. If you see the ass of him who hates you lying under its burden, you shall not pass him by: you shall surely release it with him.

Exodus 23:4-5

On Revenge

Say not: "I will do so to him as he has done to me; I will render to the man according to his work."

Proverbs 24:29

Compassion for the Enemy

If your enemy is hungry, give him bread to eat, And if he is thirsty, give him water to drink.

Proverbs 25:21

Elisha's Kindness

When the Aramean forces, sent out to capture Elisha, were themselves caught in a trap, the king of Israel said to the prophet:

"Shall I kill them, my father?"

Elisha replied:

"You must not! Would you kill those you have taken captive with your sword and bow? Set bread and water before them that they may eat and drink and go back to their master."

So the king prepared great provision for them, and when they had eaten and drunk, he sent them away and they went back to their master.

And the bands of Aram never returned to the land of Israel.

2 Kings 6:21-23

Sparing One's Enemy

Saul wept and said:

"Is that your voice, my son, David? You are more righteous than I, for you have rendered good to me, whereas I have rendered you evil . . . For if a man come upon his enemy, will he let him go unharmed?"

1 Samuel 24:18-20

EXAMPLE

Learning by Example

As Christ forgave you, forgive also.

3 Colossians 3:13

EXILE

The Native Land

Weep not for the dead,
Nor mourn for him;
But weep rather for him who goes away
Never to return
Or to see his native land again.

Jeremiah 22:10

Hope for the Despairing

The people who walked in darkness
Have seen a great light;
They who dwelt in the land of the shadow of death,
Upon them has the light shone.

Isaiah 9:1

Jeremiah's Letter

Build houses and dwell in them, and plant gardens, and eat their fruit; take wives and beget sons and daughters; and take wives for your sons, and give your daughters to husbands, so that they may bear sons and daughters, so that you may multiply there, and be not diminished. Seek the peace of the city where I have caused you to be carried away captive, and pray to the Lord for it; for in its peace shall you have peace.

Jeremiah 29:5-7

An Exiled People

Is there no balm in Gilead?
Is there no physician there? . . . . .
Oh, that my head were waters,
And my eyes a fountain of tears,
That I might weep day and night
For the slain of the daughter of my people!

Jeremiah 8:22-23

Mourning in Babylon

A voice is heard in Ramah,
Lamentation, and bitter weeping,
Rachel weeping for her children;
She refuses to be comforted for her children,
Because they are not.

Jeremiah 31:15

God's Promise to Judah and Israel

Behold, the day will come, says the Lord, when I will sow the house of Israel and the house of Judah with the seed of man and the seed of beast. And as I once watched over them to pluck up and to break down, and to overthrow and to destroy, and to harm, so I will watch over them to build and to plant, says the Lord.

In that day they shall say no more:

"The fathers have eaten sour grapes, and the children's teeth are set on edge. But only for his own iniquity shall anyone die; only the teeth of him who eats the grapes shall be set on edge."

Jeremiah 31:27-30

Isaiah's Vision
of Israel's Return

For behold, I shall create new heavens and a new earth,·
And the former things shall not be remembered,
Nor come to mind . . .
I will rejoice in Jerusalem, and exult in My people;
And the voice of weeping shall no longer be heard there,
Nor the voice of crying.
They shall build houses, and inhabit them;
They shall plant vineyards, and eat their fruit . . . .
As the years of a tree shall be the years of My people.
And My chosen shall long enjoy the work of their hands.

Isaiah 65:17-19; 21-22

God's Pledge
to the Captives

"I will gather you out of all the countries, and will bring you into your own land. A new heart will I give you, and a new spirit; I will take away your stony heart, and give you a heart of flesh. I will cause you to walk in My statutes, and keep My ordinances. You shall dwell in the land that I gave to your fathers; and you shall be My people, and I will be your God."

Ezekiel 36:24-28

After the Cleansing

In the day that I cleanse you from all your iniquities, I will cause the cities to be inhabited, and the waste places shall be rebuilt.

Ezekiel 36:33

Israel Leaving Captivity

For you shall go out with joy,
And be led forth in peace;
The mountains and the hills shall break forth into sing-
ing,
And all the trees of the field shall clap their hands.

Isaiah 55:12

FAITH

The Substance of Hope

Faith is the substance of things hoped for, the evidence of things not seen.

Hebrews 11:1

The Power of Faith

If you had faith the size of a grain of mustard seed, you could say to this sycamore tree, "Be uprooted and planted in the sea"—and it would obey you.

Luke 17:6

Unlimited Possibilities

Jesus said to him, "If you can believe, all things are possible to him who believes."

Mark 9:23

Keeping the Faith

I have fought a good fight, I have finished my course, I have kept the faith.

2 Timothy 4:7

Fate of the Unbeliever

If you will not believe, surely you shall not be established.

Isaiah 7:9

Faith, the Healer

Your faith has made you whole.

Matthew 9:22

FALSEHOOD

God's Commandment

You shall not bear false witness against your neighbor.

Exodus 20:16

On Dealing Falsely

You shall not steal, nor deal falsely, nor lie to one another.

Leviticus 19:11

False Witness

A false witness shall not be unpunished, and he who speaks lies shall not escape.

Proverbs 19:5

Spreading a Net

The man who flatters his neighbor spreads a net for his steps.

Proverbs 29:5

The Bread of Falsehood

Bread of falsehood is sweet to a man;
But afterwards his mouth shall be filled with gravel.

Proverbs 20:17

FAREWELLS

Moses Summons Joshua

Moses said to the Israelites:

"I am one hundred and twenty years old today. I am no longer able to get about easily, and the Lord has said to me that I shall not cross this Jordan . . ."

Then Moses summoned Joshua and said to him in the sight of all Israel:

"Be strong and of good courage; for you must go with this people into the land which the Lord has promised to their fathers; and you shall cause them to inherit it. It is the Lord who will march before you; He will be with you. He will not fail you, nor forsake you. So fear not, nor be dismayed!"

Deuteronomy 31:1, 7-8

The Song of Moses—
His Farewell to Israel

Moses spoke the words of this song before all the assembly of Israel:

Give ear, O heavens, and I will speak;
And let the earth hear the words of my mouth!
My doctrine shall drop as the rain,
My speech shall distil as the dew;
As the small rain upon the tender grass,
And as the showers upon the herb.
For I will proclaim the name of the Lord;
Ascribe greatness unto our God.
The Rock, His work is perfect;

For all His ways are justice . . .

Remember the days of old,
Consider the years of many generations;
Ask your father, and he will declare to you,
Your elders, and they will tell you,
How the Most High gave to the nations their inheritance,
When He separated the children of men
He set the borders of the peoples
According to the number of the children of Israel.
For the portion of the Lord is His people,
Jacob the lot of His inheritance.

He found them in a desert land,
And in the waste, a howling wilderness;
As an eagle that stirs up her nest,
Hovers over her young,
Spreads abroad her wings, takes them,
Bears them on her pinions—
So the Lord alone did lead them.

And when it is said: "Where is their god,
The rock in whom they trusted;
Who did eat the fat of their sacrifices,
And drank the wine of their drink-offering?"
Let him rise up and help you,
Let him be your protection.

See now that I, even I, am He,
And there is no god but Me;
I kill, and I make alive;
I wound, and I heal;
And there is none that can deliver out of My hand . . .

There is none like God, O Israel,
Who rides upon the heaven as your help.
The eternal God is a dwelling-place,
And underneath are His everlasting arms;
And Israel dwells in safety.
Happy are you, O Israel, who is like you?
A people savey by the Lord!

Deuteronomy 31, 32:1-4, 7; 33:26-29; 37-39

Joshua Bids Israel Farewell

Joshua called the people of Israel to Shechem and said:

"I am old and going the way of all the earth. You have seen what the Lord your God has done to all these nations, for it is He who has fought for you. Therefore keep and do all that is written in the book of the Law of Moses. Love the Lord your God. But if you join the remnant of these nations, and marry among them, they shall be a snare and a trap to you."

Joshua 23:1-3, 6-9, 11-14

FASTING

Honest Fasting

Is such the fast that I have chosen? The day for a man to afflict his soul? Is it to bow his head like a reed, and to lie in sackcloth and ashes? Will you call this a fast, a day acceptable to the Lord?

Is not this, rather, the fast that I have chosen? To loosen the fetters of wickedness, to undo the heavy burdens, and to let the oppressed go free, breaking every yoke? Is it not to share your bread with the hungry, and to shelter the homeless? When you see the naked, that you clothe him, and that you do not turn your back on your own?

Then shall your light break forth like the dawn . . . then shall you call, and the Lord will answer; You shall cry, and He will say:

"Here I am." . . .

And you shall be like a watered garden, like a spring whose waters never fail . . .

Isaiah 58:5-11

When Fasting

When you fast, do not put on a sad countenance like the hypocrites who want people to see they are fasting. When you fast, anoint your head and wash your face so that you do not appear to others to be fasting but to your Father, in secret: and your Father, who sees in secret, will reward you.

Matthew 6:16-18

FATE

Destiny Unknown

The race is not to the swift,

Nor the battle to the strong.

Ecclesiastes 9:11

FESTIVALS

The Feast of Passover

For seven days you shall eat unleavened bread, the bread of affliction, for in haste did you come forth out of the land of Egypt.

Deuteronomy 16:1, 3

Festival to the Lord

This shall be a memorial for you to keep as a festival to the Lord by all your generations . . . From the first day you shall have no leaven in your houses. On the first day you shall hold a religious assembly, likewise on the seventh day.

Exodus 12:14

The Feast of Weeks

From the time the sickle is first put to the standing corn shall you begin to number seven weeks. You shall keep the feast of weeks to the Lord your God with rejoicing, after the measure of the freewill offering which you shall give according as the Lord your God blesses you.

Deuteronomy 16:9-11

The Feast of Tabernacles

You shall keep the Feast of Tabernacles seven days, after you have gathered in from your threshing floor and winepress, and rejoice in it.

Deuteronomy 16:13-14

FOOLS

Whip, Bridle and Rod

A whip for the horse, a bridle for the ass,
And a rod for the back of fools.

Proverbs 26:3

A Foolish People

My people is foolish, they know Me not;

They are stupid children, having no understanding;
They are wise to do evil, but to do good they have no
   knowledge.

Jeremiah 4:22

A Fool's Heart

The fool has said in his heart:
"There is no God."

Psalms 14:1

FORGIVENESS

A Plea

Out of the depths have I called You, O Lord:
Lord, hear my prayer!
If You, Lord, should mark iniquities,
O Lord, who could stand?
But with You there is forgiveness . . .

Psalms 130

The Promise of Forgiveness

Says the Lord:
"Though your sins be like scarlet,
They shall be as white as snow;
Though they be red like crimson,
They shall be white as wool . . . "

Isaiah 1:18-19

The Expiation of Guilt

"Be comforted, be comforted, My people," says your
   God;
"Speak comfortingly to Jerusalem, and proclaim to her
that her service is at an end, and her guilt is expiated;
For she has received from the hand of the Lord
Double for all her sins."

Isaiah 40:1-2

Repentance and Forgiveness

If your brother trespass against you, rebuke him; and if he
repent, forgive him.

Luke 17:3

FREEDOM

The Runaway Slave

You shall not deliver to his master a bondman that is escaped from his master to you; he shall dwell with you, in the place which he shall choose within one of your gates, where it suits him best; you shall not wrong him.

Deuteronomy 23:16-17

Release from Debt

At the end of every seven years you shall make a release Every creditor shall release what he has lent his neighbor; he shall not exact it of his neighbor and his brother.

Deuteronomy 15:1-2

Release from Slavery

If your kinsmen, a Hebrew man or woman, is sold to you and serves you six years, in the seventh year you shall give him his freedom, and when you send him out free, you shall not let him go empty-handed. You shall furnish him liberally from your flock and from your threshing floor, and from your winepress, as the Lord has blessed you. For remember that you once were slaves in Egypt and the Lord your God redeemed you.

Deuteronomy 15:12-15

Liberty for All

Proclaim liberty throughout the land to all its inhabitants.

Leviticus 25:10

FRIENDSHIP

An Open Relationship

Better is open rebuke
Than love that is hidden.

Proverbs 27:5

Faithful Wounds

Faithful are the wounds of a friend;
But the kisses of an enemy are deceitful.

Proverbs 27:6

David and Jonathan

Thy love to me was wonderful, passing the love of women.

2 Samuel 1:26

A Friend's Counsel

Ointment and perfume rejoice the heart;
So does the sweetness of a man's friend by hearty counsel.

Proverbs 27:9

Sacrificing Oneself

Greater love has no man than this,
That a man lay down his life for his friends.

John 15:13

GIVING

False Friendship

Every man is a friend to him who gives gifts.

Proverbs 19:6

Giving and Receiving

It is more blessed to give than to receive.

Acts 20:35

Ability to Give

Every man shall give as he is able.

Deuteronomy 16:17

Cheerful Giving

God loves a cheerful giver.

2 Corinthians 9:7

Waiting for Tomorrow

Do not say to your neighbor: "Go, and come again and tomorrow I will give," when you have it with you.

Proverbs 3:28

Take Heed

Take heed that you do not give alms to be seen by others.

When you give alms, let not your left hand know what your right hand does.

Matthew 6:1-3

True Giving

He saw the rich men casting their gifts into the treasury, and a certain poor widow casting in two copper coins. And he said, "Of a truth I say to you that this poor widow has cast in more than all the rest: for all these have out of their abundance cast their offerings to God; but she of her penury has cast in all she owned."

Luke 21:1-4

Withholding

Withhold not good from those to whom it is due, when it is in the power of your hand to do it.

Proverbs 3:27

GLORY

Understanding God

Let not the wise man glory in his wisdom. Let not the rich man glory in his riches. But let him who glories glory in this: that he understands and knows Me.

Jeremiah 22, 23

God's Glory

The heavens declare the glory of God.

Psalms 19:1

Crown of Glory

The hoary head is a crown of glory, if it be found in the way of righteousness.

Proverbs 16:31

The Earth's Glory

Holy, holy, holy, is the Lord of hosts: the whole earth is full of His glory.

Isaiah 6:3

GOD

I Am the Lord

God said to Moses:

I am that I am.
Before Me there was no God formed,
Neither shall there be after Me.
I, even I, am the Lord;
And beside Me there is no Savior.

Isaiah 43:10-11

The First and the Last

I am He. I am the First and I am the Last.

Isaiah 44:6

Maker of the Earth

It was I who made the earth and created man upon it;
It was My hands that stretched out the heavens,
And I commanded all their host.

Isaiah 45:12

None Else

I am the Lord, and there is none else. There is no God beside Me.

Isaiah 45:5

His Face

And He said: You cannot see My face for no man shall see Me and live.

Exodus 33:w0

Invisible

No man has seen God at any time.

John 1:18

One God

There is one God; and there is none other than He.

Mark 12:32

A Still Small Voice

Elijah came to a cave, and lodged there . . . And, behold, the

Lord passed by, and a great and strong wind rent the mountains, and broke in pieces the rocks before the Lord; but the Lord was not in the wind. After the wind an earthquake; but the Lord was not in the earthquake. After the earthquake a fire; but the Lord was not in the fire; and after the fire a still small voice.

1 Kings 19:9, 11,12

God's Greatness

Then the Lord answered Job out of the whirlwind:
Where were you when I laid the foundations of the
    earth?
Declare, if you have the understanding . . .
Can you bind the chains of the Pleiades,
Or loose the bands of Orion? . . .
Who has put wisdom in the heart?
Or who has given understanding to the mind?
Will you hunt the prey for the lioness?
Or satisfy the appetite of the young lions
When they crouch in their dens
And lie in wait in their hiding place?
Know you the time when the wild goats of the rock give
    birth?
Or can you mark when the hinds calve? . . .

Job 38: 1, 4, 31, 35, 36, 39; 39:1

All Is Yours

Yours, O Lord, is the greatness and the power, and the glory, and the victory, and the majesty; for all that is in the heaven and in the earth is Yours; Yours is the kingdom, O Lord, and You are exalted as head above all.

Chronicles 29:11

Glory of God–
Dignity of Man

O Lord, our Lord,
How glorious is Your name in all the earth!
Out of the mouths of babes and sucklings
You have fashioned strength . . .
When I behold Your heavens, the work of Your fingers,
The moon and the stars, which You have established,

What is man that you should be mindful of him;
Or the son of man that You should think of him?
Yet You have made him but little lower than the angels,
And have crowned him with glory and honor.
You have given him dominion over the works of Your
  hands.
All sheep and oxen, yes, and the beasts of the field.
The birds of the air, and the fish of the sea,
Whatever swims through the paths of the seas.
O Lord, our Lord,
How glorious is Your name in all the earth!

Psalms 8:4-10

The Heavens Speak

The heavens declare the glory of God,
And the firmament shows His handiwork.
Day by day it is uttered,
Night by night the knowledge is made known;
Although there is really no speech, no words,
Nor is a voice heard.
Yet their utterance reaches throughout the earth
And their message to the ends of the world.

Psalms 19:2-5

A Thousand Generations

Know therefore that the Lord your God, He is God, the faithful God Who keeps covenant and mercy to a thousand generations with those who love Him and keep His commandments.

Deuteronomy 7:9

Righteous Judge

Shall not the Judge of all the earth do right?

Genesis 18:25

A Merciful God

The Lord God, merciful and gracious, long-suffering, and abundant in goodness and truth.

Exodus 34:6

Peter Says

Then Peter said: "Of a truth I perceive that God is no respecter of persons; but in every nation he who fears Him and works righteousness is accepted by Him.''

The Acts 10:34

Not to Be Mocked

Be not deceived: God is not mocked, for whatever man sows that also shall he reap.

Galatians 6:7

God's Power

He makes His sun to rise on the evil and on the good, and sends rain on the just and on the unjust.

Matthew 5:45

Small and Great

You shall hear the small as well as the great.

Deuteronomy 1:17

Bound or Free

Whatever good thing any man does, the same shall he receive of the Lord, whether he be bound or free.

Ephasians 6:8

Lord of Hosts

The Lord of hosts is exalted through justice and God the Holy One is sanctified through righteousness.

Isaiah 5:16

God's Mercy

When Israel was a child I loved him, and I called him out of Egypt. But the more I called him, the more he went from Me; he sacrificed to the Baalim, and made offerings to graven images. Yet is was I who taught Ephraim to walk, who held him in My arms with bands of love; Now the sword shall fall upon his cities . . . Because he will not repent. But how can I give you up, O Ephraim? How can I deliver you up, O Israel? My heart is overwhelmed, My compassion kindled. I will not give vent to the fierceness of My anger, I will not return to destroy Ephraim; For I am not man, but God, the Holy One among you. I will not destroy you!

Hosea 11:1-9

Slow to Anger

The Lord is gracious and full of compassion;
Slow to anger, and of great mercy.

Psalms 145:8

Abundant in Goodness

The Lord, the Lord God, merciful and gracious, long-suffering and abundant in goodness and truth, keeping mercy to the thousandth generation.

Exodus 34:6, 7

A Shepherd

He will feed His flock like a shepherd,
    gathering the lambs in His arms,
    carrying them in His bosom,
And gently lead those that are with young.

Isaiah 40:11

Protector of All

He who dwells in the secret place of the Most High,
And abides in the shadow of the Almighty,
Says of the Lord, "He is my refuge and my fortress,
My God, in whom I trust."
Surely He shall rescue you from the snare of the hunter
And from the horrible pestilence ...
You shall not be afraid of the terror by night,
Nor of the arrow that flies by day ...
A thousand may fall at your side,
And ten thousand at your right hand;
It shall not come near you ...
For He will give His angels charge over you,
To keep you in all your ways.
"Because he has set his love upon Me,
I will deliver him ...
He shall call upon Me, and I will answer him;
I will be with him in time of trouble;
I will rescue him ... "

Psalms 91:1-15

* * *

The Lord upholds all who fall,

And raises up all those who are bowed down.

Psalms 145:14

The Lord, Your Keeper

A Song of Ascents.
I will lift up my eyes to the mountains:
From where shall my help come?
My help comes from the Lord,
Who made heaven and earth . . .

The Lord is your keeper;
The sun shall not hurt you by day,
Nor the moon by night.
The Lord shall keep you from all evil;
The Lord shall guard your soul.
The Lord shall guard your going out and your coming in,
    from this time forth and forever.

Psalms 121

Champion of the Lowly

Who is like to the Lord our God
Who is enthroned on high,
Who looks down
Upon heaven and upon the earth below?
He raises the poor out of the dust,
And lifts the needy out of the dunghill,
That he may set him with princes,
Even with the princes of His people.
He makes the barren woman to dwell in her house
As a joyful mother of children.
Hallelujah.

Psalms 113:5-9

Unless the Lord

Unless the Lord build the house,
They labor in vain who build it;
Unless the Lord guard the city,
The watchman keeps watch in vain.

Psalms 127:1

The Rock

My God is the rock of my refuge.

Psalms 94:22

Happy People

Happy is the people whose God is the Lord.

Psalms 144

Our Refuge and Strength

God is our refuge and strength,
A very present help in trouble.
Therefore we will not fear though the earth be convulsed
  and the mountains be engulfed in the seas . . .
The Lord of hosts is with us;
The God of Jacob is our refuge!
Come, behold the works of the Lord . . .
He stops wars all over the earth;
He breaks the bow, cuts the spear to pieces;
And burns the war chariots with fire.
The Lord of hosts is with us;
The God of Jacob is our refuge!

Psalms 46

Song of Deliverance

David, son of Jesse and sweet singer of Israel, spoke the words of this song when the Lord delivered him from his enemies:

The Lord is my rock, and my fortress, and my deliverer;
The God who is my rock, in Him I take refuge;
My shield, and my horn of salvation, my high tower, and
  my refuge;
My savior, you save me from violence.
Praised, I cry, is the Lord,
And I am saved from my enemies.
For the waves of death encompassed me . . .
In my distress I called upon the Lord,
And my cry reached His ears.

2 Samuel 22:1-5, 7; 23:1

Who Is Worthy of God's Love?

Lord, who shall sojourn in Your tabernacle?

Who shall dwell upon Your holy mountain?
He who walks upright, and acts righteously.
Who speaks truth in his heart,
Who has no slander upon his tongue,
Nor does evil to his fellow man,
Nor takes up a reproach against his neighbor;
He in whose eyes a vile person is despised,
But who honors those who fear the Lord;
He who keeps his promise at all costs;
He who puts not his money out on interest,
Nor takes a bribe against the innocent.
He who does these things shall never be moved.

Psalm 15

Seven Abominable Things

There are six things that the Lord hates,
Yes, seven which are an abomination to Him:
Haughty eyes, a lying tongue,
Hands that shed innocent blood;
A heart that devises wicked schemes;
Feet that are swift in running to evil;
A false witness who breathes out lies,
And he who sows discord among brethren.

Proverbs 6:16-19

With Wings Like Eagles

Who has measured the waters of the sea in the hollow of
his hand, marked off the heavens with a span,
weighed the mountains in scales, and the hills in a
balance? . . .

To whom will you liken God?
He sits above the circle of the earth,
And its inhabitants are like grasshoppers . . .
He brings princes to nothing;
He makes the rulers of the earth as a thing of nought.

Have you not known? Have you not heard that the everlasting God, the Lord, the Creator of the ends of the
earth does not grow faint nor weary?
And there is no limit to His perception?
He gives strength to the faint;

and to the weak he gives new vigor.

Though young men shall grow faint and weary and
stumble to the ground,
Those who trust in the Lord shall renew their strength.
They shall soar with wings like the eagles;
They shall run, and not grow weary,
They shall walk forward and not grow faint.

Isaiah 40:12, 18, 22, 28-31

God Everlasting and Mortal Man

A Prayer of Moses, the man of God.

Lord, You have been our dwelling-place in all generations.
Before the mountains were brought forth, or ever You
had formed the earth and the world,
From everlasting to everlasting, You are God.
You turn man to dust, saying, "Return, O children of
men."

For a thousand years in Your sight are as yesterday
when it is past,
Or as a watch in the night...

In the morning they are like grass which sprints up.
In the morning it flourishes, and comes up;
In the evening it is cut down, and withers...

We bring our years to an end as a tale that is told.
The days of our years are three-score and ten
Or if by reason of strength fourscore years...
So teach us to number our days
That we may get us a heart of wisdom...

O satisfy us in the morning with They mercy;
That we may rejoice and be glad all our days...
And may the graciousness of the Lord our God be upon
us;
And establish upon us the work of our hands!

Psalms 90

The Grace of God

By the grace of God I am what I am: and his grace which was
bestowed upon me was not in vain; but I labored more abun-

dantly than they all; yet not I, but the grace of God which was with me.

1 Corinthians 15:10

In Praise of God

Bless the Lord, O my soul!
O Lord my God, You are very great;
You are clothed with glory and majesty ...
You established the earth upon its foundations,
That it should not ever be moved ...

You send forth springs to the valleys that sun between
   the mountains;
They give drink to every beast of the field.
The wild asses quench their thirst.
Beside them dwell the fowl of the heaven ...
You cause the grass to spring up for the cattle.
And herbs for the service of man;
To bring forth bread out of the earth;
And wine that makes glad the heart of man ...
You made the moon for the seasons;
The sun knows the time of its setting.
You make darkness, and it is night, when all the beasts
   of the forest creep forth.
The young lions roar after their prey,
And seek their food from God.
The sun rises, they slink away,
And couch in their dens.
Man goes forth to his field and to his labor until evening.

Rejoice in the Lord

How manifold are Your works, O Lord!
In wisdom have You made them all;
The earth is full of Your creatures ...
All of them wait for You to give them their food in due
   season ...
You withdraw their breath, they perish
And return to their dust ...
May the glory of the Lord endure forever;
As for me, I will rejoice in the Lord.
I will sing to the Lord as long as I live.

Psalms 104

The Holy One

In the year that King Uzziah died I saw the Lord sitting upon a throne high and lifted up. Above Him stood the seraphim; And one called to the others:

"Holy, holy, holy, is the Lord of hosts;
The whole earth is full of His glory."

Isaiah 6:1-3

* * *

You shall be holy for I the Lord your God am holy.

Leviticus 19:2

The Fatherhood of God

Have we not all one father?
Has not the one God created us?
Why do we deal treacherously every man against his
    brother,
Profaning the covenant of our fathers?

Malachi 2:10

* * *

Are you not as children of the Ethopians to Me,
O children of Israel? says the Lord.

Amos 9:7

God Our Father and Creator

But now, O Lord, you are our Father;
We are the clay, and You our Potter;
We all are the work of Your hand.

Isaiah 64:7

Omnipresent and Omniscient

For the Leader. A Psalm of David:
O Lord, You have looked into me, and You know me.
You know when I sit and when I rise,
You understand my thoughts from afar...
For there is not a word on my tongue,
But, lo, O Lord, You know it beforehand.

Where can I go from Your spirit?
Or where can I escape from Your presence?
If I ascend up to heaven, You are there;
If I make my bed in the netherworld, behold, You are
    there.
If I take the wings of the morning,
And dwell in the farthermost parts of the sea;
Even there Your hand would lead me.
And if I say: "Surely the darkness shall cover me,
And the light about me shall become night;"
Even the darkness is not dark for You,
But the night shines as the day;
Both darkness and light are the same for You . . .
Wonderful are Your works, O God!

Psalms 139:1, 4, 7-12, 14

God's Dwelling Place

Will God indeed dwell on the earth? Behold, the heaven and the heaven of heavens cannot contain You.

1 Kings 8:27

* * *

The heaven is My throne,
And the earth is My footstool;
Where is the house that you would build to Me?
And where is the place that could be My resting-place?
For all these things has My hand made . . .

Isaiah 66:1-2

* * *

Can anyone hide himself in secret places that I shall not see him? says the Lord. Did I not fill heaven and earth? says the Lord.

Jeremiah 23:24

God of Knowledge

The Lord is a God of knowledge and by Him are actions weighed.

1 Samuel 2:3

Searcher of Hearts

The Lord searches all hearts, and understands all the imaginations of the thoughts.

1 Chronicles 28:9

* * *

Can you by searching find out God?

Job 11:7

God the Omnipotent

With God all things are possible.

Matthew 19:26

* * *

I know that You can do everything.

Job 42:2

* * *

In whose hand is the soul of every living thing and the breath of all mankind?

Job 12:9-10

Who Shall Come Before God?

The earth is the Lord's, and the fulness thereof;
The world and they who dwell in it . . .
Who shall ascend to the mountain of the Lord?
And who shall stand in His holy place?
He who has clean hands, and a pure heart;
Who has not taken My name in vain,
And has not sworn deceitfully.

Psalms 24:1, 3-4

Listen to the Voice of God

"Has the Lord as great delight in burnt-offerings and sac-rifices, as in hearkening to the voice of the Lord? Behold, to obey is better than sacrifice, and to hearken than the fat of rams."

1 Samuel 15:22

The Word of God

The word of God is quick, and powerful, and sharper than any two-edged sword, piercing even to the dividing asunder of soul and spirit, and of the joints and marrow, and is a discerner of the thoughts and intents of the heart. Neither is there any creature that is not manifest in his sight: but all things are naked and opened to the eyes of him with whom we have to do.

Hebrews 4:13-14

To Stand Forever

All flesh is grass,
And all the goodliness thereof is as the flower of the
  field;
The grass withers, the flower fades;
But the word of our God shall stand forever.

Isaiah 40: 6-8

GOOD AND EVIL

Abhoring Evil

Woe to those who call evil good, and good evil; who change darkness into light and light into darkness; who change bitter into sweet, and sweet into bitter!

Isaiah 5:20

* * *

Be not overcome of evil, but overcome evil with good.

Romans 12:9

* * *

For the good that I would, I do not; but the evil which I would not, that I do.

Romans 7:19

* * *

Abhor what is evil; cleave to what is good.

Romans 12:9

* * *

Bless those who persecute you: bless, and curse not. Do not pay back evil with evil.

Romans 12:14, 17

* * *

Be not weary in well doing.

2 Thessalonians 3:13

* * *

It is better, if the will of God be so, that you suffer for well doing, than for evil doing.

Peter 3:17

Let your light so shine before men, that they may see your good works, and glorify your Father Who is in heaven.

Matthew 5:16

* * *

Be doers of the word, and not hearers only.

James 2:22

* * *

Do not withhold good from those to whom it is due, when it is in your power to do so.

Proverbs 3:27

* * *

Abstain from all appearance of evil.

Thessalonians 5:22

Jeremiah Asks

Why does the way of the wicked prosper?

Jeremiah 12:1...

Isaiah's Call

To what purpose is the multitude of your sacrifices to Me? Says the Lord: "I am full of the burnt-offerings of rams, and the fat of fed beasts: "I delight not in the blood of bullocks, or of lambs, or of he-goats. Bring me no more vain oblations; it is an offering of abomination to Me . . . When you spread out your hands, I will hide My eyes from you; when you make many prayers, I will not hear.

"Your hands are full of blood! Wash yourselves clean. Put away the evil of your doings from before My eyes, cease to do evil. Learn to do good. Seek justice, relieve the oppressed, judge the fatherless, plead for the widow."

Isaiah 1:11-17

GREED

Beware of the Greedy

My son, if sinners entice you, do not consent,
If they say, "Come with us, we shall fill our houses with
  spoil,
Cast in your lot with us; let us all have one purse,"
My son, walk not in the way with them. Restrain your foot

from their paths; for their feet run to evil.
And they make haste to shed blood,
But these lie in wait for their own blood,
They lurk for their own lives.
So are the ways of every one that is greedy of gain;

Proverbs 1:10-19

Nathan's Parable

Nathan said to the king:

"There were two men in a city: one rich, and the other poor. The rich man had many flocks and herds; but the poor man had nothing except one little ewe lamb, which he had bought and reared. She grew up with him, and with his children. She ate his own food, and drank from his own cup, and lay in his bosom. She was like a daughter to him. Now there came a traveller to the rich man, but he would not take of his own flocks and herds to prepare a meal for the traveller, but took the poor man's lamb, and prepared that for the guest.--

David was incensed at this and said:

"As the Lord lives, the man who has done this deserves to die! And he shall repay the value of the lamb fourfold, because he did this thing, and had no pity."

Nathan said: "You are the man! You have struck down Uriah the Hittite with the sword, and his wife you have taken to be your wife . . . Therefore, the sword shall never depart from your house."

. . . Then David said: "I have sinned against the Lord."

2 Samuel 12:1-13

The Commandment

You shall not covet your neighbor's house; you shall not covet your neighbor's wife, nor his man-servant, nor his maid-servant, nor his ox, nor his ass, nor anything that is your neighbor's.

Exodus 20:14

Naboth's Vineyard

Ahab spoke to Naboth the Jezreelite, saying:

"Give me your vineyard so that I may have it for a garden of herbs, since it is so close to my house. I will give you in exchange a better vineyard; or, if you like, I will give you the value of it in money."

But Naboth replied:

"The Lord forbid that I should give you the inheritance of my father!"

So Ahab went back to his house angry and dismayed because of Naboth's answer. He lay down upon his bed, turned away his face and would not eat.

Then Jezebel his wife came to him and said:

"Why are you so downcast that you are not eating?"

Ahab told her.

"Are you not the ruler of the kingdom of Israel?"

Jezebel said, "Come now. Eat, and cheer up. I will get you the vineyard."

So Jezebel wrote letters in Ahab's name, sealed them with his seal, and sent them to the elders and nobles who dwelt in the same city with Naboth.

She wrote in the letters:

"Proclaim a fast and place Naboth at the head of the people. Then let two villains face him and accuse him of having cursed God and the king. Then take him away and have him stoned to death."

The elders and nobles did just as Jezebel had commanded in the letters. They proclaimed a fast, placed Naboth at the head of the people. And the two villains came in and accused him in the presence of the people, saying, "Naboth cursed God and the King." Then they led him out of the city and stoned him to death. After this had been done, they sent word to Jezebel telling her that Naboth had been stoned to death.

When Jezebel heard this, she said to Ahab:

"Go, take possession of the vineyard Naboth refused to give you for money, since he is no longer alive."

And so Ahab went down to the vineyard of Naboth to take possession.

1 Kings 21:1-16

HAPPINESS

The Happy Man

Happy is the man whom God corrects; therefore do not despise the chastening of the Almighty.

Job 5:17

Happy is he who keeps the law.

Proverbs 29:18

`A Confused Prophet

Why, O Lord, are those who deal treacherously happy?

Jeremiah 12:1

Good and Bad Companions

Happy is the man who has not walked in the
.counsel of the wicked,
Nor stood in the way of sinners,
Nor sat in the seat of the scornful.
But his delight is in the law of the Lord;
And in His law does he meditate day and night.
He shall be like a tree planted by streams of water,
That brings forth fruit in its season.
And whose leaf does not wither;
Whatsoever he does, he shall prosper.

Not so the wicked;
They are like the chaff which the wind drives away . . .
The way of the wicked shall perish.

Psalms 1:1-4, 6

HEAVEN

Heaven Is at Hand

In those days John the Baptist preached in the wilderness of
Judea, saying:
"Repent: For the kingdom of heaven is at hand!"

Matthew 3:1-2

Entering Heaven

Not everyone who says to me, "Lord, Lord," shall enter into
the kingdom of heaven; but he who does the will of my Father
who is in heaven.

Matthew 7:21

The Urgency of
Preaching the Kingdom

A disciple said to Him:
"Lord, let me go and bury my father first."

But Jesus told him,
"Follow Me, and let the dead bury their dead."

Matthew 8:21-22

The Lord's Throne

The Lord is in his holy temple.
The Lord's throne is in heaven.

Psalms 11:4

Treasures in Heaven

Lay up for your selves treasures in heaven, where neither moth nor rust corrupts, and where thieves do not break through nor steal.

Matthew 6:20

My Father's House

"In my Father's house are many mansions . . . I go to prepare a place for you."

John 14:2

A Great Reward

Rejoice and be exceeding glad; for great is your reward in heaven; for so persecuted they the prophets who were before you.

Matthew 5:12

For the Rich: A Problem

It is easier for a camel to go through the eye of a needle than for a rich man to enter into the kingdom of God.

Matthew 19:24

For the Poor: A Blessing

Blessed be the poor: for yours is the kingdom of God.

Luke 6:20

The Kingdom of God

When his disciples rebuked those who brought young children to him, Jesus was much displeased, and said to them, "Suffer the little children to come unto me, and forbid them not: for of such is the kingdom of God."

Mark 10:14

On the Imminence
of the Kingdom

Behold the fig tree, and all the trees:

When they now shoot forth, you see and know of your own selves that summer is at hand.

So likewise, when you see these things come to pass, know that the kingdom of God is at hand.

Verily I say to you, this generation shall not pass away, till all be fulfilled.

Heaven and earth shall pass away: but not my words.

Luke 21:29-33

Parable of the Mustard Seed

The kingdom of heaven is like a grain of mustard seed, which a man sowed in his field: which indeed is the least of all seeds: but, when grown, is the greatest among herbs, and becomes a tree, so that the birds of the air come and lodge in its branches.

Matthew 13 31:32

HELL

Gates of Hell

Wide is the gate, and broad is the way, that leads to destruction; many there be who go there.

Because straight is the gate, and narrow is the way, which leads to life, few there be that find it.

Matthew 7:13, 14

Defying Hell

And I say also to you,
That you are Peter,
And upon this rock I will build my church;
And the gates of Hell shall not prevail against it.

Matthew 16:18

Chains of Darkness

God spared not the angels who sinned, but cast them down to hell, and delivered them into chains of darkness.

2 Peter 2:4

HEROINES

Deborah's Song of Victory

On that day Deborah, with Barak the son of Abinoam, sang
this song:

> Hear, O kings! Give ear, O princes!
> I will sing to the Lord;
> I will sing praise to the Lord, the God of Israel . . .

Judges 5:1-3

A Mother In Israel

> In the days of Shamgar, son of Anath,
> In the days of slavery, the highways were too dangerous
>   to travel;
> The travellers, fearful, went through byways . . .
> Until I, Deborah, arose,
> I arose, a mother in Israel . . .
> Then there was war at the gates.
> But was there a shield or spear
> Among forty thousand in Israel?

Judges 5:6-8

Call to Freedom

> Awake, awake, Deborah!
> Awake, awake, cry out!
> Arise, Barak!
> Capture your despoilers, son of Abinoam! . . .

Judges 5:12

The Tribes Rally

> The people of the Lord came and fought;
> They fought the kings of Canaan
> At Taanach by the waters of Megiddo,
> The stars too fought;
> The stars in their courses fought against Sisera.
> The brook Kishon swept them away,
> That ancient brook, the brook Kishon . . .

Judges 5:19-21

So with All God's Enemies

> So perish all Your enemies, O Lord;
> But may those who love You be as the sun rising up in all

its splendor.

Judges 5:21, 1-30

The Song of Hannah

My heart rejoices in the Lord
My horn is exalted in the Lord;
My mouth is enlarged over my enemies,
Because I rejoice in Your salvation.
There is none holy as the Lord:
For there is none beside You;
Neither is there any rock like our God . . .
Those who were well-fed have hired themselves out for
    bread,
While those who were hungry have ceased:
The Lord kills, and makes alive;
He brings down to the grave, and brings up.
The Lord makes poor, and makes rich;
He brings low, He also lifts up.
He raises up the poor out of the dust,
He lifts up the needy from the dung-hill
To seat them with princes
And inherit the throne of glory . . .
For the pillars of the earth are the Lord's,
And He has set the world upon them . . .

1 Samuel 2:1, 2, 6-8

The Song of Mary
(Also known as *The Magnificat*)

Mary said, "My soul magnifies the Lord,
My spirit rejoices in God my Savior.
For He has regarded the low estate of his handmaiden:
    behold, from henceforth all generations shall call me
    blessed.
He Who is mighty has done great things to me: and holy
    is His name.
His mercy is on those who fear Him from generation to
    generation.
He has shown strength with His arm; He has scattered
    the proud in the imagination of their hearts.
He has put down the mighty from their thrones, and
    exalted those of low degree.

He has filled the hungry with good things; and the rich
   He has sent empty away.
He has helped his servant Israel, mindful of His mercy;
As He spoke to our fathers, to Abraham, and to his
   descendants forever.

Luke 1:46-55

The Loyalty of Ruth the Moabite

Said Ruth to her mother-in-law, Naomi:
"Entreat me not to leave you and to return from following
after you; for where you go I will go; and where you lodge, I will
lodge; your people shall be my people, and your God my God;
where you die, will I die, and there will I be buried; the Lord do
so to me, and more also, if anything but death part you and
me."

Ruth 1:16-17

Esther Risks Her Life

Esther sent this reply to Mordecai:
"Go, assemble all the Jews in Shushan and have them fast
for me, neither eating nor drinking night or day for three days. I
and my maids will also fast. Then I will go to the king, although
it is contrary to the law. If I perish, I perish."

Esther 4:15-16

Abigail Pacifies David

David arose and went to the desert of Maon, where there was
a very wealthy man who owned three-thousand sheep and a
thousand goats. His name was Nabal, a churlish and tight-
fisted person, while his wife Abigail was beautiful and intelli-
gent.

When David heard that Nabal was in Carmel for the shearing
of his flock, he sent ten young men to greet him in his name and
to say:

"Peace to you and to your house and to all who belong to
you! I have just heard that you are sheep-shearing. Now when
your shepherds were with us in Carmel we did them no harm,
nor was anything of theirs ever missing. Ask your shepherds
and they will tell you. Let my young men, therefore, find favor
with you, for we have come on a feast day. And please give
them and your servant David whatever you can."

David's men delivered the message to Nabal in the name of David, and waited.

But Nabal answered:

"Who is David! Who is the son of Jesse! Nowadays there are many servants who run away from their masters. Shall I take my bread and wine and meat I have killed for my own shearers, and give it all to men who come from I know not where?"

So David's men went back and reported everything that Nabal had said.

"Let every man gird on his sword!" David cried. He did likewise and set out with about four-hundred men . . .

Meanwhile, one of Nabal's servants told Abigail what had taken place:

"David sent messengers from the desert to greet our master, but he flew at them! Actually, David's men were very good to us. We were never harmed nor did we ever miss anything as long as we were with them in the fields. They were a protection to us night and day . . . Now something must be done, for a calamity is surely in store for our master and all his house. He is such an impossible person that no one can speak to him."

Abigail hastily got together two-hundred loaves, two skins of wine, five dressed sheep, five measures of parched corn, a hundred clusters of raisins, two-hundred cakes of figs, and loaded them on asses; and she told her young men:

"Go ahead. I will follow you." But she mentioned nothing to her husband Nabal.

As she came riding down the mountain path, David and his men were coming towards her. Now David had just been saying:

"Surely it was in vain that I guarded everything this fellow had in the desert, so that nothing was missing. Now he has repaid good with evil. May God do so to David if by morning I leave a single male alive of those who belong to him!"

When Abigail saw David, she alighted, bowed before him and fell at his feet, saying:

"My lord, upon me be the blame! Let your handmaid speak and hear her out. Let not my lord pay any attention to Nabal, for he is just like his name. 'Fool' is his name and he acts like one. I, your handmaid, never saw the young men of the lord, whom you sent . . ."

Then David said to Abigail:

"Blessed be the Lord, the God of Israel, who sent you to meet me today. Blessed be your discretion and blessed be you yourself who have kept me from shedding blood and avenging myself. For, as the Lord the God of Israel lives, who has kept me from harming you, if you had not come here to meet me, by dawn there would not have been a man of Nabal's left alive."

David then accepted the gifts Abigail had brought him, and he said to her:

"Go back to your house in peace."

1 Samuel 25:1-25; 32-35

The Witch of Endor Shows Compassion

Then Saul fell full length upon the ground in fear because of Samuel's words of doom; and there was no strength left in him for he had eaten nothing all that day and night. Seeing him in such a state, the woman came to Saul and said:

"Your handmaid listened to you and put her life in your hands. Now please listen to *me*: let me set a morsel of bread before you so that you may have strength when you go on your way."

At first Saul refused, saying, "I will not eat." But his servants too urged him, and he listened to them; and soon he got up from the ground and sat upon the bed.

Meanwhile the woman killed a fatted calf she had in the house; she took flour, kneaded it and baked unleavened bread. She set all this before Saul and his servants and they ate. Then they left that same night.

1 Samuel 28:20-25

Deborah Influences Barak

Now Deborah, the prophetess, judged Israel at that time. She sat under the palm tree of Deborah in the hillcountry of Ephraim and the children of Israel came to her for judgment.

She summoned Barak, the son of Abinoam, and said to him:

"Has not the Lord commanded, saying, 'Go, march to Mount Tabor with ten-thousand Naphtilites and Zebulunites, and I will draw to you Sisera, the captain of Jabin's army at the brook Kishon, with his chariots and troops and deliver him into your hand?' "

But Barak answered:

"If you will go with me, I will go; but if you will not go with me,

I will not go."

"I will surely go with you," Deborah replied, "but the battle will not be to your glory; for the Lord will give Sisera into the hand of a woman."

And Deborah journeyed with Barak.

Judges 4:4-9

HONESTY

Honest Weights and Measures

You shall not have in your bag diverse weights, a great and a small. You shall not have in your house diverse measures, a great and a small. A perfect and just weight shall you have; a perfect and just measure shall you have.

Deuteronomy 25:13-15

* * *

Diverse weights are an abomination to the Lord;
And a false balance is not good.

Proverbs 20:23

HOPE

Job Despairs

My days are swifter than a weaver's shuttle, and are spent without hope.

Job 7:6

Substance of Hope

Faith is the substance of things hoped for, the evidence of things not seen.

Hebrews 11:1

Peter's Wisdom

Hope to the end.

1 Peter 1:13

HOSPITALITY

Welcome the Stranger

You shall have the same law for the stranger as for one of your own country.

Leviticus 24:22

The stranger who dwells with you shall be to you as one born among you, and you shall love him as yourself.

Leviticus 19:34

* * *

Be not forgetful to entertain strangers: for thereby some have entertained angels unawares.

Hebrews 13:2

Rebekah and Abraham's Servant

Rebekah came out with her pitcher upon her shoulder, and she went down to the fountain and filled it.

Abraham's servant then ran to meet her and said:

"Give me to drink, I pray you, a little water of your pitcher."

"Drink, my lord," she said, and she let down her pitcher upon her hand and gave him drink. "I will draw for your camels also," she said, "until they have done drinking."

And she emptied her pitcher into the trough and ran again to the well and drew for all his camels.

Genesis 24:15-20

HYPOCRISY

Hypocrite! First cast out the beam from your own eye; and then you shall see clearly to cast out the mote from your brother's eye.

Matthew 7:5

HUMILITY

The Meek

Blessed are the meek, for they shall inherit the earth.

Matthew 5:5

Walk Humbly

What does the Lord require of you but to do justly, and to love mercy, and to walk humbly with your God?

Micah 6:8

* * *

Whoever shall exalt himself shall be abased; and he who humbles himself shall be exalted.

Matthew 32:12

Blessed are the poor in spirit; for theirs is the kingdom of heaven.

Matthew 5:3

* * *

I dwell in the high and holy place,
With him also who is of a contrite and humble spirit,
To revive the spirit of the humble,
And to revive the heart of the contrite ones.

Isaiah 57:15

* * *

He who is least among you all, the same shall be great.

Luke 9:48

INSTABILITY

Serving Two Masters

No man can serve two masters: for either he will hate the one and love the other, or else he will hold to the one and despise the other. You cannot serve God and mammon.

Matthew 6:24

To and Fro

Be no more children, tossed to and fro, and carried about with every wind of doctrine.

Ephesians 4:14

ISRAEL

Suffering for All Nations

Surely it was our diseases that he bore,
Our pains that he carried;
While we thought him stricken,
Smitten by God, and afflicted.
But he was wounded for our transgressions . . .
And with his stripes we were healed.
We had gone astray like sheep,
Each following his own way;
And the Lord laid on him the iniquity of us all.
Yet he opened not his mouth;
As a lamb that is led to the slaughter,
And as a sheep that before her shearers is dumb,

He opened not his mouth . . .

Isaiah 53:4-7

Chosen Servant from Birth

Hear me, O isles,
Listen, O distant peoples!
The Lord called me from birth . . .
"You are My servant, Israel," He said to me,
"Through whom I show My glory."

Isaiah 49:1, 3

A Light to the Nations

"It is too little a thing," God says, "That you should be My servant to raise up the tribes of Jacob and the scattered of Israel;
"I will make you a light to the nations, that My salvation may reach to the ends of the earth."

Isaiah 49:5, 6

Do Not Fear

"But you, Israel, My servant . . .
You whom I have taken from the ends of the earth
And called from its far-off places
Fear not, for I am with you.
Be not dismayed, for I am your God.
I will strengthen you, and help you,
And uphold you with My right hand of righteousness."

Isaiah 41:8-10

A Mission to the Nations

"Behold My servant, whom I uphold:
My chosen one in whom My soul takes delight;
I have put My spirit upon him, so that he shall
bring forth justice to the nations.
He will not cry out, nor shout, making his
voice heard in the street . . .
But he shall not fail nor be discouraged
Until he brings forth justice on the earth . . ."

Isaiah 42:1-4

Israel Will Not Escape Punishment

Thus says the Lord:
For three transgressions of Israel,
Yea, for four, I will not prevent their punishment;
Because they sell the righteous for silver,
And the needy for a pair of shoes;
They trample on the head of the poor,
And turn away the humble;
And a man and his father go unto the same maid,
To profane My holy name;
And they lay themselves down beside every altar
Upon clothes taken in pledge from the poor,
And in the house of their God they drink
The wine of those who have been fined.

Amos 2:4-8

God Expects More of Israel

"You only have I known of all the families of the earth;
Therefore I will visit upon you all your iniquities."

Amos 3:2

JEALOUSY

Saul Is Jealous

When David returned from the slaying of the Philistines, the women came out of the cities of Israel, singing and dancing, to meet King Saul with songs and tambourines. They sang:

"Saul has slain his thousands,
And David his ten thousands."
And Saul was very angry.

1 Samuel 18:6-7

JERUSALEM

Jeremiah Laments the Destruction
of Jerusalem by the Chaldeans

How does the city sit solitary,
That was full of people!
How is she become as a widow! . . .
She weeps bitterly in the night,
And her tears are on her cheeks.
She has none to comfort her

Among all her lovers;
All her friends have dealt treacherously with her,
They have become her enemies.

Zion spreads forth her hands:
There is none to comfort her . . .

All who pass by clap
Their hands at you;
They hiss and wag their head
At the daughter of Jerusalem:
"Is this the city that men called
The perfection of beauty,
The joy of the whole earth?"

Lamentations 1:1-2, 17, 2:15

Wickedness in Jerusalem

Among My people are found wicked men;
They set a trap, they catch men.
As a cage is full of birds,
So are their houses full of ill-gotten gains;
Therefore they are become great, and waxen rich;
They have become fat, and sleek;
Yea, they exceed in deeds of wickedness;
They plead not the cause of the fatherless,
Nor do they defend the right of the needy.
Shall I not punish them for these things?
Says the Lord.

Jeremiah 5:26-29

The Future

Thus says the Lord of hosts:
Old men and old women, with staffs in hand shall again sit in the broad places of Jerusalem. The streets of the city shall be filled with boys and girls playing . . .

Zechariah 8:4-5

JESUS

Mary Gives Birth

Joseph went from Nazareth in Galilee to Judea — to the city of David called Bethlehem — to register for the census with Mary his espoused wife, who was big with child.

While they were there, she gave birth to her first-born son and wrapped him in swaddling clothes and laid him in a manger, because there was no room for them at the inn.

Luke 2:4-7

Legion

He asked him, "What is your name?" And he answered, saying, "My name is Legion: for we are many."

Mark 5:9

Light of the World

I am the light of the world: he who follows me, shall not walk in darkness, but shall have the light of life.

John 8:12

The Only Way to God

I am the way, the truth, and the life: no man comes to the Father, but by me.

John 14:6

His Unlimited Nature

He is the image of the invisible God, the first born of every creature: for by him were all things created that are in heaven and that are in earth, visible and invisible, whether they be thrones, or dominions, or principalities, or powers: all things were created by him, and for him.

Colossians 2:15-16

Unchangeable

Jesus Christ the same yesterday, and today, and forever.

Hebrews 13:8

How to Thank God

Whatever you do in word or deed, do all in the name of the Lord Jesus, giving thanks to God and the Father by him.

Colossians 3:17

Jesus, the Messiah

For God so loved the world, that he gave his only begotten Son that whoever believes in him should not perish, but have everlasting life.

John 3:16

Jesus Briefs His Disciples

Do not think that I have come to send peace on earth; I came not to send peace, but a sword. For I have come to set a man at variance against his father, and the daughter against her mother, and the daughter-in-law against her mother-in-law. A man's foes shall be those of his own household. He who loves father or mother more than me is not worthy of me: and he who loves son or daughter more than me is not worthy of me ...

Matthew 10:34

Jesus Enters Jerusalem

The two disciples brought the colt to Jesus and flung their garments on its back and Jesus sat on it. Many people spread their coats on the roadway, while others spread newly-cut branches on the way.

Those going before him as well as those who followed, cried out: "Hosanna! Blessed is he who comes in the name of the Lord! Blessed be the kingdom of our father David who comes in the name of the Lord! Hosanna in the highest!" And Jesus entered Jerusalem.

Mark 11:7-11

On the Cross

At the ninth hour, Jesus cried with a loud voice: "Eli, Eli, lama sabachtani!" ("My God, My God, why have You forsaken me?")

Mark 16:34

Forgive Them

Then Jesus said:
"Father, forgive them; for they know not what they do." And, finally, he cried out:
"Father, into Your hands I commend my spirit."

Luke 23:34, 46

JOY

In His Sight

God gives wisdom, knowledge and joy to the man who is

good in His sight.

Ecclesiastes 2:26

A Joyful Noise

Make a joyful noise to the Lord, all you lands!

Psalms 100:1

A Joyful Soul

I will greatly rejoice in the Lord, my soul shall be joyful in my God; for He has clothed me with the garments of salvation, he has covered me with the robe of righteousness.

Isaiah 61:10

Rejoice, Rejoice!

Rejoice in the Lord always: and again I say, Rejoice.

Philippians 4:4

Parable of the Piece of Silver

What woman having ten pieces of silver, if she should lose one of them, does not light a candle, sweep the house and seek diligently until she finds it? And when she has found it, she calls her friends and her neighbors together, saying:

"Rejoice with me: I found the silver piece I lost."

Likewise, I say to you, there is joy among the angels of God over one sinner who repents.

Luke 15:8-10

The Lost Sheep

Jesus told this parable to them:

What man of you, having a hundred sheep, if he lose one of them, does not leave the ninety and nine in the wilderness, and go after the one that he lost? And when he has found it, he lays it on his shoulders, rejoicing. And when he comes home, he calls together his friends and neighbors, saying,

"Rejoice with me. I have found the sheep that was lost!"

I say to you, that likewise there shall be more joy in heaven over one sinner who repents than over ninety and nine just persons who need no repentance.

Luke 15:3-7

JUDGMENT

Judgment Day

The day of the Lord will come as a thief in the night; in which the heavens shall pass away with a great noise, and the elements shall melt with fervent heat, the earth also and the works that are therein shall be burned up.

2 Peter 3:10, 11

The Anti-Christ and Judgment Day

That day shall not come, except there come a falling away first, and that man of sin be revealed, the son of perdition; who opposes and exalts himself above all that is called God, or that is worshipped; so that he as God sits in the temple of God, showing himself that he is God.

2 Thessalonians 2:3-4

JUSTICE

God Warns Unjust Judges

Defend the poor and the fatherless;
Do justice to the afflicted and destitute.
Rescue the poor and needy;
Deliver them out of the hand of the wicked.

Psalms 82:3-4

Equality Under Law

You shall have the same law for the stranger as for the home-born.

Leviticus 24:22

Remember Your Redemption

You shall not pervert the justice due to the stranger or to the fatherless; nor take the clothes of a widow as a pledge. Remember that you were a slave in Egypt, and the Lord your God redeemed you from there.

Deuteronomy 24:17-18

Judging Righteously

You shall do no unrighteousness in judgment; you shall not be partial to the poor, nor favor the person of the mighty; but in righteousness shall you judge your neighbor.

Leviticus 19:15

How Absalom, David's Son, Stole the Loyalty of the People

Absalom prepared a chariot and horses and fifty men to run before him. He would rise up early and stand alongside the road to the gate. When anyone had a lawsuit to take to the king for judgment, Absalom would call to him and say: "What city are you from?" When the answer came, "Your servant is from this or that tribe of Israel," Absalom would say to him: "Your case is good and just; but there is no one appointed by the king to hear you. Oh, that I were appointed a judge — so that every man with a suit might come to me and I would see that he received justice!"

When any person came by and bowed before him, Absalom would put out his hand and take hold of him and kiss him. Behaving in this manner to all Israelites who came to the king for judgment, Absalom stole the hearts of the men of Israel.

2 Samuel 15:1-6

Denouncing the Corrupt Judge

They abhor whoever speaks honestly,
They afflict the just, take bribes
And turn aside the needy at the gate.
They have turned justice into gall,
And the fruit of righteousness into wormwood.

Amos 5:6

Amos Pleads

Seek good, and not evil, that you may live;
Then the Lord, the God of hosts, will be with you.
Hate evil, love good,
And establish justice at the gate.

Amos 5:14-15

KINDNESS

God's Kindness

According to the kindness that I have done to you, you shall do to me.

Genesis 21:23

Brotherly Love

Be kindly affectioned one to another with brotherly love; in honor preferring one another.

Romans 12:19

Regarding the Beast

A righteous man regards the life of his beast; But the tender mercies of the wicked are cruel.

Proverbs 12:10

David's Blessing

Word had come to David that the men of Jabesh-Gilead had buried Saul; and so he sent messengers to these men saying:

"May you be blessed by the Lord for having shown this kindness to your lord Saul and burying him. Now may the Lord be kind and true to you. I also will repay you for your kindness for having done this. Be courageous and strong! Although your lord Saul is dead, the people of Judah have anointed me king over them.

2 Samuel 2:4-7

LABOR

The Value of Work

In all labor there is profit.

Proverbs 14:23

Justice in Labor

The laborer is worthy of his hire.

Luke 10:7

* * *

Masters, give to your servants what is just and equal.

Colossians 4:1

Invitation to the Careworn

Come to me, all who labor and are weary and I will give you rest.

Matthew 11:28

Dust to Dust

In the sweat of your face shall you eat bread, till you return to the ground . . . for dust you are and to dust you shall return.

Genesis 3:19

A Sabbath

Six days shall you labor and do all your work.

Deuteronomy 5:13

On Weariness

All things toil to weariness . . .

Ecclesiastes 1:8

On Indolence and Industry

Go to the ant, you sluggard;
Consider her ways, and be wise;
Which having no chief,
Overseer, or ruler,
Provides her bread in the summer,
And gathers her food in the harvest.
How long will you sleep, O sluggard?
"Yet a little sleep, a little slumber,
A little folding of the hands to sleep"
So shall your poverty come as a thief,
And your want as an armed man.

Proverbs 6:6-11

Taking Away Necessary Work-Tools

No man shall take a mill or upper millstone to pledge; for he takes a man's life to pledge.

Deuteronomy 24:6

Paying Proper Wages

Woe unto him who builds his house by unrighteousness,
And his chambers by injustice;
Who uses his neighbor's service without wages,
And gives him not his hire.

Jeremiah 22:13

LEADERSHIP

Honesty in Government

He who rules over men must be just.

2 Samuel 23:3

When the righteous are in authority, the people rejoice; But when the wicked rule, the people despair.

The Leader's Attributes

Render to Caesar the things that are Caesar's, and to God the things that are God's.

Mark 12:17

The True Ruler

Then the men of Israel said to Gideon:
"Rule over us, both you and your son, and your son's son; for you have saved us from the Midianites.
But Gideon replied:
"I will not rule over you, neither shall my son rule over you; the Lord shall rule over you."

Judges 8:22-23

Israel Demands a King

"You are old, and your sons don't walk in your ways; now make us a king to rule us like the other nations."

Samuel 8:5, 20

Samuel's Warning

The prophet Samuel warned them:
"This will be the manner of the king that shall reign over you: he will take your sons, and make them his horsemen and his captains and to till his ground, and to reap his harvest, and to make his instruments of war. He will make your daughters become his perfumers, cooks and bakers. He will take your fields and your vineyards, and your oliveyards. He will take a tenth of your flocks; and you will be his servants."
But the people refused to listen to Samuel.

1 Samuel 8:11-19

Making Oneself Understood

If the trumpet give an uncertain sound, who shall prepare himself to the battle?

1 Corinthians 14:8

Blind Leading the Blind

Can the blind lead the blind? Shall they not both fall into

the ditch?

Luke 6:39

LIGHT

The Lord Is Light

The Lord is my light and my salvation.

Psalms 27:1

The Law Is Light

The commandment is a lamp, and the law is light.

Proverbs 6:23

Light of Life

I am the light of the world: he who follows me shall not walk in darkness but shall have the light of life.

John 8:12

LOVE

As Strong As Death

For love is strong as death;
Jealousy is cruel as the grave ...
Many waters cannot quench love.

Song of Songs 8:6, 7

A Time to Love

A time to embrace, and a time to refrain from embracing.
A time to love, and a time to hate.

Ecclesiastes 3:5, 8

Love vs. Hatred

Better is a dinner of herbs where love is,
Than a fatted ox and hatred with it.

Proverbs 15:17

Love Your Enemies

Love your enemies, bless those who curse you, do good to those who hate you, and pray for those who despitefully use you, and persecute you.

Matthew 5:44

Love the Stranger

The stranger that sojourns with you shall be to you as one born among you, and you shall love him as yourself.

Leviticus 19:34

* * *

Love you therefore the stranger; for you were strangers in the land of Egypt.

Deuteronomy 10:19

God and Love

Hear, O Israel: The Lord our God, the Lord is one. And you shall love the Lord your God with all your heart, and with all your soul, and with all your might. And these words, which I command you this day, shall be upon your heart; and you shall teach them diligently to your children, and shall talk of them when you sit in your house, and when you walk by the way, and when you lie down, and when you rise up. And you frontlets [philacteries] between your eyes. And you shall write them upon the doorposts of your house, and upon your gates.

Deuteronomy 6:4-9

* * *

Whom the Lord loves he chastens.

Hebrews 12:6

* * *

He who loves not knows not God; for God is love.

1 John 4:8

* * *

This is the love of God, that we keep his commandments.

1 John 5:3

* * *

If we love one another, God dwells in us, and his love is perfected in us.

1 John 4:12

Love for Israel

The Lord did not set His love upon you, nor chose you, because you were more in number than any people — for you were the fewest of all peoples. It was because the Lord loved you, and would keep the oath which He swore to your fathers;

therefore has the Lord brought you out with a mighty hand, and redeemed you out of the house of bondage, from the hand of Pharaoh king of Egypt. Know, therefore, that the Lord your God is a faithful God who keeps His covenant and mercy for a thousand generations to those who love Him and follow His commandments.

Deuteronomy 7:7-9

Better than Wine

The song of songs, which is Solomon's.
Let him kiss me with the kisses of his mouth —
For your love is better than wine.

Song of Songs 1:

A Lily Among Thorns

I am a rose of Sharon,
A lily of the valley.
As a lily among thorns,
So is my love among the daughters.

Song of Songs 2:1-2

Love Your Neighbor

You shall love your neighbor as yourself.

Leviticus 19:18

* * *

All the law is fulfilled in one word, even in this: you shall love your neighbor as yourself.

Galatians 5:14

* * *

Jesus answered: "The first of all the commandments is: Hear, O Israel! The Lord our God is one Lord! And you shall love the Lord your God with all your heart, and with all your soul, and with all your mind, and with all your strength: this is the first commandment.
"The second is: you shall love your neighbor as yourself."
"There is no other commandment greater than these."

Mark 12:29-31

Jesus to His Disciples

"A new commandment I give to you, that you love one

another as I have loved you."

John 13:34

Love and Friendship

Greater love has no man than this, that he lay down his life for his friends.

John 15:13

MARRIAGE

The Positives of Marriage

It is not good that man should be alone.

Genesis 2:18

* * *

What God has joined together, let not man put asunder.

Matthew 19:6

* * *

It is better to marry than to burn.

1 Corinthians 7:9

* * *

For this cause shall a man leave his father and mother and shall be joined to his wife, and the two shall be one flesh.

Ephesians 5:31

Marital Sharing

A wife does not own her own body, but her husband does. Likewise, a husband does not own his own body; his wife does.

1 Corinthians 7:4

* * *

Men ought to love their wives as their own bodies. He who loves his wife loves himself.

Ephesians 5:28

Samson Would Marry a Philistine

When Samson told his father and his mother that he had seen a Philistine woman in Timnah whom he wished to have as his wife, they said:

"Is there no woman among the daughters of our own people, that you must take a wife from the heathen Philisines?"

Samson answered:

"Get her for me. She pleases me."

. . . Then Samson and his parents went down to Timnah and, behold, a young lion came roaring at him. But the spirit of the Lord came upon him and he tore the young lion to pieces as one would have torn a kid.

Judges 14:2-3, 5-6

MEDITATION

What to Meditate On

Whatever things are true, whatever things are honest, whatever things are just, whatever things are pure, whatever things are lovely, whatever things are of good report . . . think of these things.

Philippians 4:8

His Law

His delight is in the law of the Lord,
And in His law does he meditate day and night.

Psalms 1:2

MERCY

A Merciful God

When you are in trouble, and all these things have come upon you, finally, if you turn to the Lord your God, and are obedient to His voice — for the Lord your God is a merciful God — He will not forsake you, nor destroy you, nor forget the covenant of your fathers which He swore to them.

Deuteronomy 4:30-31

Mercy Saves

Not by works of righteousness which we have done, but according to His mercy He saved us.

Titus 3:5

Live Mercifully

Let not mercy and truth forsake you: bind them about your neck; write them upon the table of your heart.

Proverbs 3:3

* * *

With the Merciful You show Yourself merciful.

2 Samuel 22:26

* * *

Blessed are the merciful, for they shall obtain mercy.

Matthew 5:7

Hosea Speaks

For I desire mercy, and not sacrifice, and the knowledge of God rather than burnt-offerings.

Hosea 6:6

Mercy, Not Sacrifice

I will have mercy, and not sacrifice: for I am not come to call the righteous, but sinners to repentance.

Matthew 9:13

Mercy for the Murderer

The Lord put a mark on Cain, lest anyone finding him should kill him.

Genesis 4:15

Cities of Refuge

The Lord said to Joshua:

"Speak to the children of Israel, saying: Assign cities of refuge ... that a man who kills another without meaning to and without hatred, may flee there; and they shall be your places of refuge from the next of kin who might try to avenge the slain man. Even though the avenger pursues him, they shall not deliver up the slayer who killed unintentionally ... "

And six cities in various parts of the land were designated cities of refuge.

Joshua 20:1-3, 5, 7-9

Micah Reminds Us

With what shall I come before the Lord, and bow myself before God on High? Shall I come before Him with burnt-offerings, with calves a year old? Will the Lord be pleased with thousands of rams, with ten thousand rivers of oil? Shall I give my first-born for my transgression, the fruit of my body for the sin of my soul?

It has been told you, O man, what is good, and what the

Lord requires of you: Only to do justly, and to love mercy, and to walk humbly with your God.

Micah 6:6-8

MESSIANIC AGE

God's Promise of Peace

In that day I will make a covenant for them with the beasts of the field, and with the fowls of heaven,
And with the creeping things of the ground;
And I will break the bow and the sword and the battle out of the land,
And I will betroth you to Me forever;
Yes, I will betroth you to Me in righteousness, and in justice,
And in lovingkindness, and in compassion,
And I will betroth you to Me in faithfulness;
And you shall know the Lord.

Hosea 2:20-22

* * *

The wolf shall dwell with the lamb ... and a little child shall lead them.

Isaiah 11:6

God's New Covenant

"Behold, I will make a new covenant with the house of Israel, and with the house of Judah. I will put My law within them, and in their hearts will I write it; and I will be their God, and they shall be My people."

Jeremiah 31:31-33

The Day of Forgiveness

Mercy and truth shall meet;
Righteousness and peace will kiss each other.
Truth shall spring out of the earth;
And righteousness shall look down from heaven.

Psalms 85:11-12

The Time of the Messiah

May the king judge Your people with righteousness and Your poor with justice.
May he judge the poor, save the children of the needy, and

crush the oppressor . . .

For he will rescue the needy when he cries for help, and the poor and the helpless.

He will redeem them from oppression and violence.

And precious will their blood be in His sight.

Psalms 72:4, 12-14

*   *   *

And there shall come forth a shoot out of the stock of Jesse,
And a twig shall grow forth out of his roots.
And the spirit of the Lord shall rest upon him,
And the spirit of wisdom and understanding,
The spirit of counsel and might,
The spirit of knowledge and of the fear of the Lord.
He shall not judge after the sight of his eyes,
Neither decide after the hearing of his ears;
But with righteousness shall he judge the poor,
And decide with equity for the meek of the land;
He shall smite the land with the rod of his mouth,
With the breath of his lips shall he slay the wicked.
Righteousness shall be the girdle of his loins,
And faithfulness the girdle of his reins.

Isaiah 11:1-9

*   *   *

Even nature will be at peace.
The wolf shall dwell with the lamb,
And the leopard shall lie down with the kid;
And the calf and the young lion and the fatling together;
And a little child shall lead them.
And the cow and the bear shall feed;
Their young ones shall lie down together;
And the lion shall eat straw like the ox.
And the sucking child shall play on the hole of the asp,
And the weaned child shall put his hand in the basilisk's den.
They shall not hurt nor destroy
In all My holy mountain;
For the earth shall be full of the knowledge of the Lord,
As the waters cover the sea.

Isaiah 11:6-9

Micah's Vision

But they shall sit every man under his vine and under his

fig-tree;
And none shall make them afraid.

Micah 4:1-4

Swords Into Plowshares

The word that Isaiah saw concerning Judah and Jerusalem.
It shall come to pass in the end of days,
That the mountain of the Lord's house shall be established as
   the highest of the mountains,
And shall be exalted above the hills;
All nations shall flow to it.
And many peoples shall go and say:

   "Come, let us go up to the mountain of the Lord,
   To the house of the God of Jacob;
   That He will teach us His ways,
   And we will walk in His paths."

For out of Zion shall go forth the law,
And the word of the Lord from Jerusalem.
He shall judge between the nations,
And shall decide for many peoples;
And they shall beat their swords into plowshares,
And their spears into pruning hooks;
Nation shall not lift up sword against nation,
Neither shall they learn war any more.

Isaiah 2:2-4

MIRACLES

God Regrets Creating Man

When the Lord saw how great was man's wickedness on earth and how every desire of man was evil, He regretted having made man and His heart was grieved. So the Lord said: "I will blot out from the earth the men whom I have created; also, the beasts, and creeping things and birds of the air . . . " But Noah found favor in the eyes of the Lord.

Genesis 6:5-8

The Flood

In the six hundredth year of Noah's life . . . all the fountains of the deep broke up and the windows of heaven were opened . . . Noah and his sons, Shem, Ham and Japheth, and Noah's wife and the three wives of Noah's sons, entered the ark, together with every beast after its kind, all cattle after their kind and every kind of creeping thing on earth, every kind of bird. Those entering were male and female, two of every species, as God had commanded Noah. Then the Lord shut him in.

The flood continued on the earth for forty days and nights. As the waters rose, they lifted the ark above the earth . . . and the mountains were covered . . . and all flesh perished that moved upon the earth . . . The Lord blotted out every living thing on the face of the earth. Only Noah and those with him in the ark were left.

Genesis 7:13-23

* * *

After a hundred and fifty days the waters decreased. The ark rested in the seventh month, on the seventeenth day of the month, upon the mountains of Ararat . . . Noah again sent the dove out of the ark . . . and the dove returned in the evening, in her mouth an olive-leaf freshly plucked; so Noah knew that the waters had abated from the earth.

Genesis 8:10-12, 3-4

God's Promise

The Lord said in His heart:

"I will never again curse the ground because of man; for the imagination of man's heart is evil from his youth . . . While the earth remains, seedtime and harvest, cold and heat, summer and winter, and day and night shall not cease."

Genesis 8:21-22

* * *

"I have set my bow in the cloud," God said, "and it shall be for a token of a covenant between Me and the earth . . . waters shall never again become a flood to destroy all flesh.

Genesis 9:13-15

Jacob Struggles With an Angel

Jacob was left alone and a man wrestled with him until dawn. When the man saw that he could not prevail over him, he struck the hollow of his thigh so that Jacob's thigh was strained. Then the man said: "Let me go; it is daybreak." But Jacob said: "I will not let you go until you bless me."

"What is your name?" the man asked. He replied, "Jacob." Then the man said: "You shall no longer be called Jacob but Israel, for you have struggled with God and with men, and have prevailed." And he blessed him.

Genesis 32:25-30

A Pillar of Salt

But Lot's wife looked back from behind him and she became a pillar of salt.

Genesis 19:26

Sodom and Gomorrah

The Lord caused brimstone and fire to rain upon Sodom and Gomorrah.

Genesis 19:24

Out of the Burning Bush

The angel of the Lord appeared to Moses in a flame of fire out of a bush: and as he looked, the bush was on fire but was not consumed.

Exodus 3:2

Staff Becomes a Snake

Moses and Aaron went to Pharaoh and did as the Lord had commanded: Aaron threw down his staff before Pharaoh and his servants, and it became a snake. Pharaoh then called upon his magicians and sorcerers, who did likewise through their secret arts . . . but Aaron's staff swallowed up their staffs.

Exodus 7:10-12

The Tenth Plague . . . and the Exodus

It came to pass at midnight that the Lord struck down all the firstborn in the land of Egypt . . . and there was a great wailing in Egypt for there was not a house where someone was not dead. Pharaoh now summoned Moses and Aaron and said:

"Rise up, leave my people, both you and the children of Israel and serve the Lord as you have demanded! Take your flocks and your herds and be gone! . . . " The Egyptians too urged the people to make haste and go for they feared that otherwise they would all die.

So the people took their dough before it was leavened, with

their kneading-troughs wrapped up in their clothes upon their shoulders. And they did according to the word of Moses: they asked the Egyptians for jewels of silver and gold, and for clothing . . . And the Egyptians let them have whatever they asked for . . .

Exodus 12:29-36

Pillar of Cloud, Pillar of Fire

The Lord went before the Israelites by day in a pillar of cloud, to lead the way; and by night in a pillar of fire, to give them light. Thus they could journey by day and by night.

Exodus 13:21

Moses Divides the Red Sea

Moses stretched out his hand over the sea; and the Lord caused the sea to go back by a strong east wind through the night and made the sea dry land. Once the water was divided the children of Israel walked into the midst of the sea on the dry ground; and the water was like a wall for them on their right hand and on their left.

The Egyptians pursued them into the midst of the sea, all of Pharaoh's horses, his chariots and his horsemen . . .

Then Moses stretched out his hand over the sea; and by morning the water returned and covered the chariots and the horsemen of Pharaoh's entire army that had followed the Israelites; not one of them escaped . . .

Exodus 14:21-28

Exodus from Egypt: A Psalm

When Israel came forth out of Egypt,
The house of Jacob from a people of strange language;
Judah became His sanctuary,
Israel His dominion.

The sea saw it, and fled;
The Jordan turned back.
The mountains skipped like rams,
The hills like young sheep.

What ails you, O sea, that you flee?
O Jordan, that you turn back?
You mountains, that you skip like rams?
You hills, like young sheep? . . .

Psalms 114:1-6

God Feeds the Israelites

Now the children of Israel grumbled against Moses and Aaron. They said:

"Would that we had died by the hand of the Lord in the Land of Egypt, while we had our fleshpots and plenty to eat! But you had to bring us to this wilderness and starve us!"

Then the Lord said to Moses:

"I will cause bread from heaven to rain down upon you. The people shall go out every day and gather a day's portion. On the sixth day they shall gather bread for two days, since the seventh day is the sabbath I have given them for a solemn day of rest . . ."

And so . . . in the morning there was a layer of dew around the camp. When the dew evaporated, there on the ground lay flakes like hoarfrost . . .

"This is the bread the Lord is giving you," Moses told the people. "Let every man gather according to the needs of the family in his tent . . ."

The Israelites called the food Manna. It was like coriander seed, only white, and tasted like wafers made with honey.

The children of Israel ate the Manna for forty years, until they came to the inhabited land of Canaan.

Exodus 16:2-5, 13-15, 35

The Brazen Serpent

When the fiery serpents were biting the people and many of them were dying, the people came to Moses and said:

"We have sinned, because we complained against the Lord and you. Pray to the Lord that he take the serpents away from us."

So Moses prayed for the people and the Lord said to Moses:

"Make a metal serpent and set it upon a pole; and whenever anyone is bitten, let him look at it, and he shall recover."

Moses thereupon made a serpent of brass and set it upon a pole; and whenever anyone bitten by a serpent looked at this brazen serpent, he recovered.

Numbers 21:6-9

God Answers Elijah's Prayer

Elijah came near and said:

"O Lord, God of Abraham, of Isaac, and of Israel, let it be known this day that You are God in Israel, and that I am Your servant, and I have done all these things at Your word . . . "

Then the fire of the Lord consumed the burnt-offering, and the wood, and the stones, and the dust, and licked up the water that was in the trench. When all the people saw it, they fell on their faces; and cried out:

"The Lord, He is God! The Lord, He is God!"

1 Kings 37-39

The Lord Aids Joshua

Then spoke Joshua:

"Sun, stand still upon Gibeon;

And you, Moon, in the valley of Aijalon!"

And the sun stood still and the moon stayed until the nation had avenged themselves on their enemies.

Joshua 10:12-13

Elijah to Heaven in a Chariot of Fire

As they talked there appeared a chariot of fire, and horses of fire, which parted them; and Elijah went up by a whirlwind to heaven . . . and Elisha took the mantle of Elijah that fell from him.

2 Kings 2:11-14

Feeding a Multitude

Now when Elisha came to Gilgal there was a famine in the land and someone from Baal-Shalisha brought the man of God twenty loaves of barley. Elisha said: "Give it to the people to eat." His servant answered: "How can I set this before a hundred men?"

"Give it to the people to eat, for thus says the Lord: 'They shall eat and shall have something left over.' "

So he set it before the hundred men and they ate; and there was something left over, as the Lord had said.

2 Kings 4:38, 42-44

Elisha and the Shunamite's Son

When Elisha came into the house, the child lay dead upon his bed. Elisha shut the door and prayed to the Lord. He lay upon the child, put his mouth upon his mouth, his eyes upon his eyes, his hands upon his hands; he stretched himself upon him; and the child grew warm. Then . . . the child opened his eyes.

2 Kings 4:32-35

Naaman is Cured

Elisha sent word to Naaman, who had become a leper, saying: "Go and wash in the Jordan seven times and your flesh will heal and you shall be clean."

Naaman, the captain of the Aramean army, was furious:

"I thought he would surely come out to me, and call on the Lord his God, and wave his hand over me to cure me," he said. "Are not the rivers of Damascus, the Amanah and Pharper, better than all the waters of Israel? Why could I not wash in them and be clean?" And he rode away in a rage.

But his servants came to him and said:

"My father, if the prophet had bid you do some great and difficult thing, would you not have done it? All the more, then, when he says to you, 'Wash and be clean.' "

Naaman then went and washed seven times in the Jordan, as the man of God had told him; and his flesh became like the flesh of a little child, and he was clean again.

2 Kings 5:10-14

Jesus Helps a Blind Man

A man who was blind from birth said:

"A man called Jesus made clay and anointed my eyes and said to me: 'Go to the pool of Siloam and wash.' I went and washed, and I received sight."

John 9:11

Jonah and the Whale

The Lord prepared a large fish to swallow up Jonah; and Jonah was in the belly of the fish three days and three nights. Then Jonah prayed to the Lord his God out of the belly of the fish . . .

The Lord then spoke to the fish, and it vomited out Jonah upon the dry land.

Jonah 2:1-2, 11

Daniel's Friends Survive the Fiery Furnace

When the three officials, Jews, were brought before the king, Nebuchadnezzar said to them:

"Is it true, O Shadrach, Meshach and Abednego, as certain Chaldeans have charged, that you do not serve my gods, nor worship the great golden statue I have set up? Now when you hear the sound of the trumpet, pipe, harp, psaltery, bagpipe and other instruments, you must fall down and worship my golden statue. If you do not, you shall be cast into a burning fiery furnace. And who is the god that can deliver you out of my hands?"

Shadrach, Meshach and Abednego answered:

"We have no need to answer you about this. If our God whom we serve can deliver us from the fiery furnace and out of your hand, O king, we pray He will! But if He does not, O king, know that we still will not serve your gods, nor worship your golden statue."

Nebuchadnezzar turned livid with rage. He ordered the furnace heated seven times hotter than usual; and several husky soldiers bound the three in their cloaks and tunics and cast them into the fiery furnace. And so hot was the furnace that the flames slew the soldiers who had cast in Shadrach, Meshach and Abednego. But the three men fell down, bound, in the midst of the burning furnace.

Then Nebuchadnezzar the king was astonished at what he saw, and he said:

"Did we not cast three men, bound, into the fire?"

"Truly, O king."

"But I see four men," he said, "walking in the fire, unbound and unhurt. And the fourth is like a son of the gods!"

Nebuchadnezzar then went near the mouth of the burning furnace, and cried out:

"Shadrach, Meshach and Abednego, servants of God the Most High, come out!"

Shadrach, Meshach and Abednego then came out of the fire. And the satraps, the prefects, and the governors, and the king's ministers saw that the fire had no power over the bodies of these men. Not a hair of their heads was singed nor were their cloaks changed, nor was there a smell of fire on them.

Nebuchadnezzar said:

"Blessed be the God of Shadrach, Meshach and Abednego, who has sent His angel and delivered His servants who trusted in Him and disobeyed the king's command and yielded their bodies so that they might not serve nor worship any god except their own God . . ."

Then the king promoted Shadrach, Meshach and Abednego in the province of Babylon.

Daniel 3:12-30

The Handwriting on the Wall

Belshazzar the king made a banquet for a thousand of his lords . . . Then they brought the gold and silver vessels that had been taken from the temple at Jerusalem; and the king and his lords, his consorts and his concubines drank from them. As they drank they praised their own gods of gold and silver, of brass and iron, of wood and stone.

Suddenly the fingers of a man's hand were seen writing against the candlestick on the plaster of the wall, and the king saw the palm of the hand that wrote. The king turned white and his thoughts terrified him so that his joints trembled and his knees knocked together . . .

All the king's wise men were called in, but they could not read the writing nor tell what it meant. King Belshazzar was terror-stricken . . .

Now the queen came into the banquet house and said:

"O king, live forever. Do not be alarmed. There is a man in your kingdom named Daniel, in whom is the spirit of the holy gods; and in the days of your father he was found to have understanding and surpassing wisdom . . . Let Daniel be sent for and he will tell you what the writing means."

So Daniel was brought before the king, who said to him:

"Are you Daniel of the Jewish captivity, whom my father the king brought out of Judah? I have heard that the spirit of the gods is in you and that you have understanding and surpassing wisdom. Now if you can read the writing and make known to me its meaning you shall be clothed in purple and have a chain of gold about your neck and you shall rule as one of three in the kingdom."

Then Daniel answered the king:

"Let your gifts be for yourself and give your rewards to another. Nevertheless, O king, I will read the writing for you and tell you what it means. The Most High God gave your father Nebuchadnezzar the kingdom with greatness, glory and majesty. Because of the greatness He gave, the people and nations of all languages trembled and feared him. Whomever he would, he slew and whomever he would, he kept alive; whomever he would, he raised and whomever he would, he put down. But when his heart grew too proud and his spirit hardened into arrogance, he was deposed from his kingly throne and his glory was taken from him; he was driven from among men and he was made to become like a beast, and his dwelling was with wild asses; he ate grass like an ox; his body was wet with the dew of heaven; until he learned that it is the Most High God who rules the kingdom of men and sets up over it whomever He will.

"You his son, O Belshazzar, have not humbled your heart, though you knew all this; you have arrogated yourself against the Lord of heaven. You brought the vessels of His temple before you; and your lords, your consorts, and your concubines have drunk wine from them while praising gods of silver and gold, of brass and iron, wood and stone, which see not, nor hear, nor understand. But the God in whose hand your breath is and everything you do, you have not praised. From Him was the palm of the hand sent, and the writing.

"This is what was inscribed:
MENE, MENE, TEKEL, UPHARSIN.

And this is what the words mean: MENE, God has numbered the days of your kingdom and brought it to an end; TEKEL, you are weighed in the scales and found wanting; UPHARSIN, your kingdom is divided and given to the Medes and Persians."

. . . That night Belshazzar the Chaldean king was slain.

Daniel 5

Daniel and the Lions

After a sleepless night, King Darius rose very early in the morning and hastened to the den of lions. When he came near, he cried out in anguish:

"O Daniel, servant of the living God, has your God whom you serve continually been able to deliver you from the lions?"

Daniel said to the king:

"O king, live forever! My God has sent His angel and he has shut the lions' mouths so that they have not hurt me."

Daniel 6:19-23

The Angel and the Shepherds

There were shepherds living in the field, keeping watch over their flocks by night when, lo, an angel of the Lord appeared to them and the glory of the Lord shone around them.

"Do not fear," the angel said to them, "for I bring you good tidings of great joy, which shall be to all people. For in the city of David this day is born to you a Savior who is Christ the Lord. This shall be a sign to you: you will find the infant in a manger wrapped in swaddling clothes.

Suddenly there was with the angel a multitude of the heavenly host praising God and saying:

"Glory to God in the highest, and on earth peace, good will toward men."

Luke 2:4-8-14

Fulfillment of Prophecy

Now all this was done, that it might fulfill what was spoken by the Lord through the prophet, saying:

"Behold, a virgin [young woman] shall be with child and bear a son and they shall call his name Emmanuel, meaning, God is with us."

Matthew 1:22-23

The Wise Men and the Birth of Jesus

Now when Jesus was born in Bethlehem of Judaea in the days of Herod the king, there came wise men from the east to Jerusalem, saying:

"Where is he who is born King of the Jews? For we have seen his star in the east and have come to worship him."

Matthew 2:1-2

The Wise Men Follow the Star

When they had heard the king, they departed and lo, the star which they saw in the east went before them till it came and stood over where the young child was. When they saw the star they rejoiced exceedingly.

Matthew 2:9-10

The Wise Men Bring Jesus Gifts

When the wise men came into the house, they saw the young child with Mary his mother, and fell down and worshipped him.

They they opened their treasure chests and presented him with gifts of gold, frankincense and myrrh.

Matthew 2:11

The Wise Men Do Not Report the Child To Herod

Being warned by God in a dream that they should not return to Herod, they departed to their own country by another way.

Matthew 2:12

Walking On Water

In the fourth watch of the night Jesus went to them, walking on the sea.

Matthew 14:25

Two Fish and Five Loaves

Jesus commanded the multitude to sit down on the grass and took the five loaves and two fish, and looking up to heaven, he blessed and broke them and gave the loaves to his disciples who passed them on to the crowd. And they were all fed; and the fragments that remained filled twelve baskets. Those who had eaten were about five thousand, besides women and children.

Matthew 14:19-21

MOSES

How Moses Was Saved

When Jochebed could no longer hide her three-month-old child at home, she made him a basket of bulrushes daubed with lime and pitch. She put the baby in it and laid it among the reeds by the river Nile's edge. His sister, Miriam, watched from a distance to see what would happen to him.

Now the daughter of Pharaoh came down to bathe in the river while her maids walked along the river bank. Suddenly she saw the basket among the reeds and sent her maid to fetch it. She opened it and saw a child, a baby, crying.

She said:

"Ah, this is one of the Hebrews' children."

Then his sister said to Pharaoh's daughter:

"Shall I go and call you a nurse from among the Hebrew women, to nurse the child for you?"

"Yes, do," she said.

So the girl went and called the child's own mother.

Pharaoh's daughter said to her:

"Take this child away and nurse it for me, and I will pay you wages."

So the woman took the child and nursed it. When the child grew she brought him to Pharaoh's daughter and he became like her son. She called him Moses, "Because I drew him out of the water." Exodus 2:3-10

Moses on Mt. Sinai

In the third month, after the children of Israel left Egypt, they came to the wilderness of Sinai. There Israel encamped at the foot of the mount while Moses went up to the mountain to God. Then the Lord called out to him:

"Tell this to the Israelites: You have seen what I did to the Egyptians and how I bore you on eagle wings and brought you here. Therefore, if you will hearken to My voice and keep My covenant, you shall be My special treasure among peoples . . . You shall be to Me a kingdom of priests, a holy nation. Now tell this to the children of Israel."

So Moses went and summoned the elders of the people. When he laid before them all that the Lord had spoken to him, the people all answered together:

"Everything that the Lord has said, we will do!"

Exodus 19:1-8

The Giving of the Law

On the morning of the third day, there was thunder and lightning and a thick cloud upon the mount, and a very loud trumpet blast, so that all the people in the camp trembled. Moses then led them out of the camp to meet God; and they stood at the foot of the mountain. Mount Sinai was wrapped in smoke, since the Lord descended upon it in fire; the smoke arose like smoke from a furnace and the mountain quaked violently. The trumpet blast grew louder and louder as Moses spoke and God answered him . . .

Exodus 19:16-19

Moses Helps the Daughters of Jethro

One day while Moses was sitting by a well in Midian the

seven daughters of the local priest, Jethro, came to draw water for their father's flock. Some shepherds began driving them away but Moses came to their defense, then helped the women water their flock.

When they came home, their father said:

"How is it you are home so early today?"

They replied:

"An Egyptian protected us from the shepherds. And he drew water for us and watered our flock."

"Where is he?" said Jethro. "Did you just leave him? Invite him to eat with us."

Moses went home with them and lived with them. Later Jethro gave him his daughter, Zipporah, to marry.

Exodus 2:15-22

Moses Rescues a Slave

When Moses was grown he went out among his people, observing them at their hard labor. One day he came upon an Egyptian taskmaster flogging an Israelite. Moses looked around and when he did not see anyone watching him he struck down the Egyptian, then hid his body in the sand.

Next day he went out again and came upon two Israelites quarreling. Moses said to the one in the wrong:

"Why did you strike your brother?"

Replied the man:

"Who made you a ruler and judge over us? Are you thinking of killing me as you killed the Egyptian?"

Then Moses was afraid, realizing that what he had done was known. And when Pharoah learned about it, he did seek to have Moses put to death. But Moses escaped from Pharaoh and fled to the land of Midian.

Exodus 2:11-15

The Lord Calls Moses

When the Lord saw that Moses came over to see why the burning bush was not consumed, God called to him from the bush: "Moses! Moses!"

He said, "Here I am."

God said: "Come no closer; remove the shoes from your feet, for the place where you are standing is holy ground. I am the God of your father, the God of Abraham, the God of Isaac, and the God of Jacob."

Moses hid his face; for he was afraid to look at God.

The Lord continued: "I have seen the affliction of my people in Egypt and have heard their cry because of their taskmasters; so I know their pain. I have come to deliver them out of the land of the Egyptians and to bring them out of that land to a good and spacious land, a land flowing with milk and honey . . . Come, now! I will send you to Pharaoh to lead My people, the children of Israel, out of Egypt."

But Moses said to God: "Who am I, that I should go to Pharaoh and lead the children of Israel out of Egypt?"

Exodus 3:4-11

Moses' Speech Difficulty

Moses said to the Lord:

"Oh Lord, I am not a man of words . . . for I am slow of speech and tongue."

The Lord replied:

"Who has made man's mouth? Or who makes a man dumb, or deaf, or seeing, or blind? Is it not I, the Lord? Now therefore, go! I will help you speak and teach you what you must say."

Exodus 4:10-12

MOURNING

The Lord Shall Comfort

Sing, O heavens; and be joyful, O earth;
And break forth into singing, O mountains;
For the Lord has comforted His people,
And will have mercy upon His afflicted.

Isaiah 49:13

* * *

Blessed are they who mourn: for they shall be comforted.

Matthew 5:4

MURDER

Planning a Murder

Then David wrote a letter to Joab, captain of his army, and sent it by the hand of Uriah, saying:

"Place Uriah in the front line of the hottest battle, and leave him so that he may be struck down."

2 Samuel 11:15

David Kills Goliath

"You come to me with sword, and spear, and javelin; but I come to you in the name of the Lord of hosts, the God of the armies of Israel, whom you have taunted. This day the Lord will deliver you into my hand . . . that all the earth may know that the Lord saves not with sword and spear."

. . . And David put his hand to his bag, and took out a stone; he slung it, and it struck the Philistine on his forehead, and he fell on his face to the earth. David ran over to the Philistine, drew his sword out of the sheath, and slew him. And when the Philistines saw that their mighty champion was dead, they fled.

1 Samuel 17:32, 37-40, 43-46, 49-51

Pharaoh's Decree

Pharaoh then charged all his subjects:

"Throw every Hebrew son who is born into the river — although you may let the new-born daughters live."

Exodus 1:22

Slaughter of the Innocents

When Herod saw that he was mocked by the Wise Men, he became furious. He ordered the slaying of all children two years and under in and around Bethlehem.

Matthew 2:16

NATURE

God's Creation

God saw everything that he had made, and behold, it was very good.

Genesis 1:31

The Lord's Earth

The earth is the Lord's, and the fulness thereof;
The world, and they who dwell therein.

Psalms 24:1

Heavens and the Firmament

The heavens declare the glory of God,
And the firmament shows His handiwork.

Psalms 19:1

The Beauty of Flowers

Think of the flowers growing in the fields: They never have to work or spin: yet I assure you that not even Solomon in all his regalia was robed like one of these.

Matthew 6:28-29

The Holy Mountain

They shall not hurt nor destroy
In all My holy mountain:
For the earth shall be full of the knowledge of the Lord,
As the waters cover the sea.

Isaiah 11:9

A Sabbath for the Fields

You shall hallow the fiftieth year, and . . . it shall be a jubilee to you; you shall not sow, neither reap what grows of itself, nor gather the grapes in it of the undressed vines.

Leviticus 25:10-11

Earth and Man

He is God who formed the earth and made it; He created it not for waste; He formed it to be inhabited.

Isaiah 45:18

Poem of Spring

For lo, the winter is past,
The rains are over and gone.
The flowers appear on the earth,
The time of singing has come,
And the voice of the turtle is heard in our land.
The fig tree puts forth her green figs,
And the vines in blossom give forth their fragrance.
Arise, my love, my beautiful one, and come away!

The Song of Songs 2:11-13

NEIGHBORS

You and Your Neighbor

Let your foot be seldom in your neighbor's house;
Lest he be sated with you, and hate you.

Proverbs 25:17

* * *

Withhold not good from the needy
When it is in the power of your hand to do it.
Say not to your neighbor: "Go, and come again,
Tomorrow I will give"; when you have it to give.
Devise not evil against your neighbor,
Seeing he dwells trustingly by you.

Proverbs 3:27-29

* * *

Better is a neighbor that is near than a brother far off.

Proverbs 27:10

* * *

You shall not hate your brother in your heart; . . . You shall not take vengeance, nor bear any grudge against him, but you shall love your neighbor as yourself.

Leviticus 19:17-18

Your Neighbor's Vineyard

When you come into your neighbor's vineyard, then you may eat grapes until you have enough at your own pleasure; but you shall not put any in your vessel.

When you come into your neighbor's standing corn, then you may pluck ears with your hand; but you shall not move a sickle into your neighbor's standing corn.

Deuteronomy 23:25-26

OPPRESSION

You Were Strangers

You shall neither vex a stranger, nor oppress him, for you were strangers in the land of Egypt.

Exodus 22:21

A Refuge

The Lord also will be a refuge for the oppressed, a refuge in times of trouble.

Psalms 9:9

Freedom for the Oppressed

Is not this the fast that I have chosen? To loose the bands of wickedness, to undo the heavy burdens, and to let the oppressed go free?

Isaiah 58:6

* * *

You shall not oppress one another.

Leviticus 25:14

The Fate of Oppressors

The wicked have drawn out the sword, and have bent their bow to cast down the poor and needy, to slay such as are upright.

But their swords shall enter their own hearts, and their bows shall be broken.

Psalms 37:14-15

PARENTS

The Commandment

Honor your father and your mother.

Exodus 10:12

Advice to Parents and Children

Fathers, do no provoke your children to anger, lest they be discouraged.

Colossians 3:21

* * *

Learn first to show piety at home.

1 Timothy 5:4

* * *

Hearken to your father who begot you, and despise not your mother when she is old.

Proverbs 23:22

Mother, Father and Me

He who loves father or mother more than me is not worthy of me.

Matthew 10:37

* * *

Children, obey your parents in the Lord: for this is right. Honor your father and mother; which is the first commandment with promise.

Ephesians 6:1-2

David, On Learning of Absalom's Death

"Is young Absalom safe?" the king asked.

The messenger answered: "May the enemies of my lord the king, and all who rise up to harm you, be as that young man is!"

Then the king, much moved, went up to the chamber over the gate, and wept. And as he went, he cried:

"O, my son Absalom, my son, my son Absalom! Would I had died instead you, O Absalom, my son, my son!"

2 Samuel 18:31-32; 19-1

A Parent's Influence

As the mother is, so is her daughter.

Ezekiel 16:44

PATIENCE

Patience and Man

Be patient toward all men.

1 Thessalonians 5:14

Waiting Patiently

Trust in the Lord, and wait patiently for Him.

Psalms 37:7

Coming of the Lord

Be patient for the coming of the Lord . . . Take the prophets who have spoken in the name of the Lord for an example of suffering and patience.

James 5:7-10

Suffering Patiently

What glory is it if when you are punished for your faults you take it patiently? But if you patiently suffer for doing the right thing this is acceptable to God.

1 Peter 2:20

PEACE

Paths of Peace

"Her [the Torah's] ways are ways of pleasantness and all her paths are peace."

Proverbs 3:17

Peace in the Priestly Blessing

"The Lord will give strength to His people: the Lord will bless His people with peace."

Psalms 29:11

Peace on Earth

Glory to God in the highest, and on earth peace, good will toward men.

Luke 2:14

Peaceable Living

If it be possible, as much as lies in you, live peaceably with all men.

Romans 12:18

God's Peace

The peace of God, which passes all understanding.

Philippians 4:7

False Peace

They have healed the hurt of my people slightly, saying, "Peace, peace," when there is no peace

Jeremiah 6:14

Peace and Quiet

Better is a dry morsel in peace,
Than a house full of feasting with strife.

Proverbs 17:1

Righteousness Brings Peace

The work of righteousness shall be peace;
And the effect of righteousness, quietness and confidence
   forever.

Isaiah 32:17

The Reward of Righteousness

And Asa (king of Judah) did what was good and right in the eyes of the Lord his God . . . and he had no war in those years, because the Lord had given him rest.

2 Chronicles 14:1, 5

Pursue Peace: Do Good

Depart from evil and do good:
Seek peace and pursue it.

Psalms 34:14

Peace With the Enemy

When a man's ways please the Lord, he makes even his enemies at peace with him.

God Ends War

God makes wars to cease to the end of the earth:
He breaks the bow and cuts the spear asunder;
He burns the chariots with fire.

Psalms 46:9-10

The Perfect Man

Mark the perfect man, and behold the upright: for the end of that man is peace.

Psalms 37:37

Prince of Peace

His name shall be called . . . The Prince of Peace.

Isaiah 9:6

Peacemakers

Blessed are the peacemakers: for they shall be called children of God.

Matthew 5:9

Peace or a Sword?

Think not that I have come to send peace on earth: I came not to send peace, but a sword.

Matthew 10:34

PERFECTION

The Lord's Perfection

You shall be perfect with the Lord your God.

Deuteronomy 18:13

* * *

Be perfect even as your Father who is in Heaven is perfect.

Matthew 5:48

* * *

If we love one another, God dwells in us, and his love is perfected in us.

1 John 4:12

Treasure in Heaven

"All these things (the Commandments) have I kept from my youth," the young man said to Jesus. "What do I lack?"

"If you would be perfect, go and sell what you have and give it to the poor, and you shall have treasure in heaven: then come and follow me."

But when the young man heard that, he went away sorrowfully, for he had great possessions.

Matthew 19:20-22

POVERTY

The Lord Objects

"What do you mean by beating my people to pieces, and grinding the faces of the poor?" says the Lord of hosts.

Isaiah 3:15

Blessed in Spirit

Blessed in spirit are the poor: for theirs is the kingdom of heaven.

Matthew 5:3

Dependable

The poor always you have with you.

John 12:8

Honoring God

He who oppresses a poor man insults his Maker,
But he who is kind to the needy honors God.

Proverbs 14:31

Deaf Ears

He who stops his ears at the cry of the poor
Shall himself cry out but shall not be answered.

Proverbs 21:13

Mocking the Maker

Those who mock the poor blaspheme their Maker.

Proverbs 17:5

Pledges and the Poor

When you lend your neighbor any manner of loan, you shall not go into his house to fetch his pledge. You shall wait outside until the man to whom you have lent shall bring the pledge outside to you. If he is a poor man, you shall not sleep in the garment he gives you as a pledge; you shall surely restore it to him by sunset so that he himself may sleep in it.

Deuteronomy 24:10-13

Defend the Poor

Defend the poor and fatherless; do justice to the afflicted and needy.

Psalms 82:3

The Stranger, Fatherless and Widow

When you reap your harvest in your field, and have forgotten a sheaf in the field, you shall not go back to fetch it; it shall be for the stranger, for the fatherless, and for the widow.

When you beat your olive-tree, you shall not go over the boughs again; it shall be for the stranger, for the fatherless, and for the widow.

When you gather the grapes of your vineyard, you shall not glean it after yourself; it shall be for the stranger, for the fatherless, and for the widow.

Deuteronomy 24:19-22

Shutting Out the Poor

Woe unto those who join house to house,

Who connect field to field,
Till there is no room, and you are made to dwell
Alone in the midst of the land!

Isaiah 5:8

PRAYER

Secret Prayer

When you pray, enter your room and when you have shut your door, pray to your Father in secret; and your Father who sees in secret shall reward you openly.

Matthew 6:5-6

The Father Knows

Your Father knows what things you have need of, before you ask Him.

Matthew 6:8

Teach Us

Lord, teach us to pray.

Luke 11:1

One for Another

Confess your faults one to another, and pray one for another, that you may be healed. The effectual fervent prayer of a righteous man avails much.

James 5:15-16

Hannah Prays Silently

As Hannah prayed, Eli the priest, who sat by the doorpost of the temple of Shiloh, watched her mouth. Now Hannah spoke in her heart; her lips moved but her voice could not be heard. Therefore Eli thought she was drunk, and he said to her:
"How long will you be drunken? Put away your wine."
Hannah said:
"No, my lord, I am a woman of sorrowful spirit; I have drunk neither wine nor strong drink, but I poured out my heart before the Lord. Do not think me wicked, for I have been speaking out of my grief."
Then Eli said: "Go in peace, and may God grant what you have asked of Him."

1 Samuel 1:1-17

Solomon Dedicating His Temple

"Concerning the stranger who is not of Your people Israel ... when he shall come and pray toward this temple, hear him from Your heavenly dwelling place."

1 Kings 8:41-43

Joshua's Prayer
In the Presence of All Israel

"O Sun, stand still upon Gibeon!
And you, Moon, in the valley of Aijalon!"

Joshua 10:12

Samson's Prayer Before
Bringing Down the Temple of Dagon

"O Lord God, remember me! Strengthen me this once, O God, that I may be avenged of the Philistines for my two eyes ... Let me die with the Philistines."

Judges 16:28, 30

Worshiping a False God

They took the bullock and dressed it and called on the name of Baal from morning until noon, saying:

"O Baal, answer us!" But there was no answer. And they leaped about the altar.

When it was noon Elijah mocked them, saying: "Cry louder for he is a god. Either he is musing or he has gone out; or he is on a journey, or perhaps he is sleeping and must be awakened."

1 Kings 18:26-27

Elijah's Prayer at Carmel

When it was time to offer the evening sacrifice, Elijah came near and said:

"O Lord, God of Abraham, of Isaac, and of Israel, let it be known this day that You are God in Israel, and that I am Your servant and have done all these things at Your command. Hear me, O Lord! Hear me, that this people may know that You, Lord, are God ... "

And the fire of the Lord consumed the offering.

1 Kings 18:36-37

The Sailors' Prayer

After the prophet Jonah told the sailors to throw him into the raging sea, they cried to the Lord:

"We beseech You, let us not perish for taking this man's life, and do not charge us with shedding innocent blood; for You, O Lord, have done as You saw fit."

Jonah 1:14

Jonah's Prayer

"Out of my distress I called to the Lord and He answered me.

"Out of the belly of the netherworld I cried for help and You heard my voice . . . "

Jonah 2:1-3

Prayer of Jesus' Disciples at Sea

And, behold, there suddenly arose a tempest in the sea, so that the ship was covered with the waves: but Jesus was a-sleep. So his disciples woke him, saying: "Lord, save us! We shall perish!"

Matthew 8:24-25

Praying at Length

Jesus went out to a mountain to pray, and continued all night in prayer to God.

Luke 6:12

Jonah's Angry Prayer

Displeased and angry when the people of Nineveh turned from their evil ways and God did not punish them, Jonah prayed:

"O Lord, was not this why I fled to Tarshish? I knew that You are a gracious God, compassionate, long-suffering, abounding in mercy, and loathe to punish. Therefore, O Lord, please take my life; for it is better for me to die than to live."

Jonah 4:1-4

Jesus to His Disciples

I say to you, ask, and it shall be given you; seek, and you shall find; knock, and it shall be opened to you.

For everyone who asks receives; and he who seeks finds;

and to him who knocks it shall be opened.

If a son should ask bread of any of you who is a father, would he give him a stone? Or if he asked for a fish, would he give him a serpent?

Or if he should ask an egg, would he offer him a scorpion?

If you then, being evil, know how to give good things to your children, how much more will your heavenly Father give the Holy Spirit to those who ask Him!

Luke 11:9-13

Seek and You Shall Find

If you seek the Lord your God with all your heart and soul, you shall find Him.

Deuteronomy 4:29

"The Lord's Prayer"

Our Father in heaven, hallowed be Your name.

Your kingdom come. Your will be done on earth as it is in heaven.

Give us this day our daily bread,

And forgive us our debts as we forgive our debtors.

Lead us not into temptation, but deliver us from evil: for Yours is the kingdom, and the power, and the glory, forever. Amen.

Matthew 6:9-13

God's Promise to the Exiles in Babylon

"When you look for Me, you will find Me. Yes, when you seek Me with all your heart, you will find Me."

Jeremiah 29:13-15

The Power of Prayer

"Ask, and you will receive. Seek, and you will find. Knock, and it will be opened to you. For anyone who asks, receives; anyone who seeks, finds; anyone who knocks, enters."

Matthew 7:7-11

The Lord Is Near

The Lord is near to all who call upon Him,

To all who call upon Him in truth.

Psalms 145:18

The Priestly Blessing

The Lord told Moses to speak to Aaron and his sons, and tell them: "This is the way you shall bless the children of Israel, saying:

The Lord bless you, and keep you;

The Lord make His face to shine on you and be gracious to you;

The Lord lift up His countenance on you, and give you peace."

Numbers 6:24-26

Prayer for Acceptance

Let the words of my mouth and the meditation of my heart be acceptable before You,

O Lord, my Rock, and my Redeemer.

Psalms 19:15

The Beatitudes

Jesus came down the mountain with them and stood in the plain in the company of his disciples and a great multitude of people from all Judea and Jerusalem and the seacoast of Tyre and Sidon, people who came to hear him and be healed of their diseases.

He lifted up his eyes to his disciples and said:

Blessed are you poor, for yours is the kingdom of God.

Blessed are you who hunger now, for you shall be filled.

Blessed are you who weep now, for you shall laugh.

Blessed are you when men shall hate you and when they shall separate you from their company, and shall reproach you and cast out your name as evil, for the Son of Man's sake.

Rejoice in that day and leap for joy: for, behold, your reward shall be great in heaven: for in like manner did their fathers behave to the prophets.

. . . I say to you who hear: Love your enemies, do good to those who hate you.

Bless those who curse you and pray for those who treat you badly.

To him who strikes you on the one cheek, offer also the other; and to him who takes away your cloak, let him have your coat also . . .

As you would that men should do to you, do also to them. For if you love those who love you, what great thing is that? For sinners also love those who love them. And if you do good to those who do good to you, what credit is in it for you? Sinners too do that.

And if you lend to those from whom you hope to be paid back, what merit is there in that? Sinners also lend to sinners, expecting to receive payment.

But love your enemies, and do good; and lend, hoping for nothing in return, and your reward shall be great, and you shall be the children of the Highest. For He too is kind to the unthankful and to the wicked.

Be merciful, therefore, as your Father also is merciful.

Do not judge and you will not be judged: do not condemn and you will not be condemned. Forgive and you shall be forgiven.

Give and it shall be given to you; good measure, pressed down and shaken together and running over, shall men give into your bosom. For the same measure that you mete out will be measured back to you.

Luke 6:17-38

Seeking God

As the heart pants for the water of the brook,
So my soul pants for You, O God.
My soul thirsts for God, for the living God ...

Psalms 42:1-3

PREACHING

The Scriptures

All scripture is given by inspiration of God, and is profitable for doctrine, for reproof, for correction, for instruction in righteousness: That the man of God may be perfect, thoroughly furnished on all good works.

1 Timothy 3:16-17

Preaching the Word of God

Preach the word constantly, in season and out of season: patiently reproving, rebuking and exhorting.

2 Timothy 4:2

*   *   *

How beautiful are the feet of those who preach the gospel of peace, and bring glad tidings of good things!

Romans 10:15

PRIDE

Pride Goes

Pride goes before destruction, and a haughty spirit before a fall.

Proverbs 16:18

Exhalting Oneself

Whoever shall exalt himself shall be abased; and he who shall humble himself shall be exalted.

Matthew 23:12

Equality

He who is greatest among you, let him be as the younger; and he who is chief, as he who serves.

Luke 22:26

Man or God?

The word of the Lord came to me, saying:
"Son of man, say to the prince of Tyre;
You have said, 'I am a god, I sit in the seat of God.' Yet you are a man, and not a god . . . Strangers shall bring you down to the pit to die. Will you still say before him who slays you: 'I am a god?' You are a man, and not a god."

Ezekiel 28:1-28-9

PROPHETS

Man of Strife

Woe is me, my mother, that you have borne me, a man of strife and a man of contention to the whole earth.

Isaiah 15:10

False Prophets

Beware of false prophets, who come to you in sheep's clothing, but inwardly are ravening wolves.

Matthew 7:15

Not Without Honor

Jesus said to them:
A prophet is not without honor, except in his own country, among his own kin, and in his own house.

Mark 6:4

Prophets Are Examples

Take, my brethren, the prophets, who have spoken in the name of the Lord, for an example of suffering, affliction, and of patience.

James 5:10

* * *

Like people, like priest.

Hosea 4:9

The Prophet Sees

Your sons and your daughters shall prophesy.
Your old men shall dream dreams.
Your young men shall see visions.

Joel 3:1

False Prophet and False Priest

Far from the least of them to the greatest,
Every one is greedy for gain;
And from the prophet to the priest
Every one deals falsely.
They have healed also the hurt of My people lightly,
Saying: "Peace, peace", when there is no peace.
Yet they are not at all ashamed,
Neither know they how to blush.

Jeremiah 6:13-15

Amos Retorts to Amaziah

"O you seer, go!" cried Amaziah, Priest of Beth-El, "Flee to the land of Judah and earn your living prophesying there; but never again prophesy at Beth-El, for this is the king's sanctuary and a royal house."
Then answered Amos:
"I was no prophet but . . . the Lord told me to prophesy . . . Now hear the word of the Lord:

You say not to prophesy against Israel,
Nor preach against the house of Isaac.
Now thus says the Lord:
Your wife shall be a harlot in the city,
Your sons and your daughters shall fall by the sword,
Your land shall be divided;
You yourself shall die in an unclean land,
And Israel shall surely be led away captive! . . . "

Amos 7:12-17

The Urgency of Prophesying Now

The lion has roared!
Who will not fear?
The Lord God has spoken!
Who can but prophesy?

Amos 3:8

The Nature of Prophecy

No prophecy of the scripture is of anybody's private interpretation. The prophecy of old came not by someone's willing it; but, rather, holy men of God spoke as they were moved by the Holy Spirit.

2 Peter 1:20, 21

In the Messianic Time

Your sons and daughters shall prophesy, your old men shall dream dreams, your young men shall see visions.

Joel 2:28

Anointed

The Lord has anointed me to teach good tidings.

Isaiah 61:1

Ordained

I ordained you a prophet to the nations.

Jeremiah 1:5

* * *

God Calls Amos

I was no prophet, nor a prophet's son; I was a herdsman and a dresser of sycamore trees. The Lord took me from caring for the flock and said to me: "Go, prophesy to My people Israel."

Amos 7:12-15

Isaiah Answers

I heard the voice of the Lord saying, "Whom shall I send? And who will go for us?"

Then I said, "Here am I, send me."

Isaiah 6:8, 9

Jeremiah is Chosen

The word of the Lord came to me, saying: "Before I formed you in the belly I knew you, And before you came out of the womb I sanctified you; I have appointed you a prophet to the nations."

Then I said: "O Lord, God! I cannot speak: for I am but a youth." But the Lord said to me:

"Say not, I am a youth; for to whomever I shall send you you shall go, and whatever I shall command you, you shall speak. Do not be afraid of them; for I am with you to deliver you."

Then the Lord put forth His hand, and touched my mouth; and said to me:

"Behold, I have put My words in your mouth; I have this day set you over the nations and over the kingdoms, to root out and to pull down, to destroy and to overthrow; to build and to plant."

Jeremiah 1:4-10

PURITY

On Being Pure

With the pure You will show Yourself pure.

2 Samuel 22:27

* * *

Shall a man be pure before his Maker?

Job 4:17

* * *

Blessed are the pure in heart: for they shall see God.

Matthew 5:8

* * *

To the pure all things are pure.

Titus 1:15

REBUKE

An Excellent Oil

Let the righteous smite me; it shall be a kindness; and let him reprove me: it shall be an excellent oil for my head.

Psalms 141:5

The Scorner, the Wise Man

Reprove not a scorner, lest he hate you: Rebuke a wise man and he will love you.

Proverbs 9:8

The Goodness of Affliction

It is good for me that I have been afflicted; that I might learn Your statutes.

Psalms 119:7

Endure Chastening

Do not despise the chastening of the Lord nor faint when you are rebuked by Him: for whom the Lord loves he chastens . . . If you endure chastening, God deals with you as with sons: for what son is there whom his father does not chasten?

Hebrews 12:5-7

REDEMPTION

The Good Shepherd

I am the good shepherd: the good shepherd gives his life for the sheep.

John 10:10

Eternal Redemption

Neither by the blood of goats and calves, but by his own blood he entered the holy place, having obtained eternal redemption for us.

Hebrews 9:12

Follow Me

Whoever will come after me let him deny himself and take up his cross and follow me.

Mark 8:34

REPENTANCE

The Prophet Despairs

Can the Ethiopian change his skin,
Or the leopard his spots?
Then may you also do good,
Who are accustomed to do evil.

Jeremiah 13:23

The Lord's Pleasure

"Have I any pleasure at all that the wicked should die?" says the Lord God, "and not rather that he should return from his ways and live?"

Ezekiel 18:23

New Heart, New Spirit

Cast away from you all your transgressions ... and make yourself a new heart and a new spirit; for why should you die, O house of Israel?

Ezekiel 18:31

Return to the Lord

Let the wicked forsake his way, and the unrighteous man his thoughts; and let him return to the Lord, and He will have mercy upon him, and to our God, for He will abundantly pardon.

Isaiah 55:7

Heaven at Hand

Repent, for the kingdom of heaven is at hand!

Matthew 3:2

Call to Sinners

I came not to call the righteous, but sinners to repentance.

Mark 2:7

Joy in Heaven

Joy shall be in heaven over one sinner who repents, more than over ninety and nine just persons who need no repentance.

Luke 15:7

Promise of Forgiveness

"If the wicked man turns from the sins he has committed and keeps My statutes and do what is lawful and right, he shall surely live, he shall not die. None of his transgressions shall be held against him."

Ezekiel 18:21-22

God Wants Repentance

"Yet even now," says the Lord "turn to Me with all your heart . . . Rend your hearts and not your garments. For the Lord, your God is gracious and compassionate, longsuffering, abounding in mercy, and relenting . . . "

Joel 2:12-14

David's Prayer of Repentance

A Psalm of David, when Nathan the prophet came to him and denounced him for taking Bath-sheba, another man's wife, as his own:

"I acknowledge my transgressions;
And my sin is ever before me.
I have done what is evil in Your sight . . .
Create in me a clean heart, O God;
And renew a steadfast spirit within me."

Psalms 51:5-6, 12

God Spares the People of Nineveh

When God saw by their actions how they turned from their wicked ways, He repented of the evil that He had threatened to do to them.

Jonah 3:10

RESPONSIBILITY

Responsibility for One's Own Conduct

Fathers shall not be put to death for their children, neither shall the children be put to death for their fathers.

Deuteronomy 24:16

* * *

Everyone of us shall give account of himself to God.

Romans 4:12

If you were blind, you should have no sin: but now you say, we see; therefore your sin remains.

John 9:41

* * *

You only have I known of all the families of the earth; therefore I will visit upon you all your iniquities.

Amos 3:2

My Brother's Keeper?

"Where is Abel your brother?" the Lord asked Cain.
He answered: "I do not know. Am I my brother's keeper?"

Genesis 4:9

The Twins, Jacob and Esau

The Lord said to Rebekah, wife of Isaac:
"Two nations are in your womb ... one shall be stronger than the other, and the older shall serve the younger."

Genesis 25:23

RESURRECTION

Coming Alive

As in Adam all die, even so in Christ shall all be made alive.

1 Corinthians 15:22

Raising the Dead

Why should it be thought incredible that God should raise the dead?

Acts 26:8

At the Second Coming

The dead in Christ will rise first: then we who remain and are alive, shall be caught up with them in the clouds, to meet the Lord in the air: and so we shall be with the Lord forever.

1 Thessalonians 4:16-17

The Sleeping Awake

Many of those who sleep in the dust of the earth shall awake, some to everlasting life, and some to everlasting shame and contempt. But the wise shall shine as the brightness of the firmament: and those who guide the many to righteousness shall be like the stars for ever and ever.

Daniel 12:2-3

I Am

I am the resurrection, and the life; he who believes in me, though he were dead, yet shall he live;
Whoever lives and believes in me shall never die.

John 11:25-25

REWARD

Receiving Your Just Reward

He who does wrong shall receive for the wrong he has done: and there is no favoritism.

Collossians 3:25

*   *   *

According to their deeds, He will repay.

Isaiah 59:18

*   *   *

He shall reward every man according to his works.

Matthew 16:27

*   *   *

Love your enemies and do good; and lend, hoping for nothing again; and your reward shall be great ...

Luke 6:35

*   *   *

Do not be deceived: God is not mocked, for whatever a man sows, that he also reaps ... Let us not grow weary of doing good, for in due season we shall reap our harvest.

Galatians 6:7, 9

*   *   *

Cast your bread upon the waters,
For you shall find it after many days.

Ecclesiastes 11:1

RIGHTEOUSNESS

Abraham Pleads With God

Abraham said: "Will You indeed sweep away the righteous with the wicked? Suppose there are fifty righteous persons

within the city of Sodom?... or forty-five?... Forty?...
Thirty?... Twenty?... What if only ten righteous persons?"
God replied: "For the sake of those ten, I will not destroy it."

Genesis 18:23-32

The Righteous Shall Flourish

The righteous shall flourish like the palm-tree;
He shall grow like a cedar in Lebanon.

Psalms 92:13

RIGHTEOUSNESS

Thoughts About Righteousness

Open to me the gates of righteousness.

Psalms 118:9

*   *   *

Let your priests be clothed with righteousness.

Psalms 132:9

*   *   *

Let righteousness run as a mighty stream.

Amos 5:24

*   *   *

The wicked flee when no one pursues;
The righteous are bold as a lion.

Proverbs 28:1

*   *   *

Righteousness exalts a nation;
But sin is a reproach to any people.

Proverbs 14:34

Statutes and Ordinances of Righteousness

The Lord spoke to Moses, saying: Speak to all the congregation of the children of Israel, and say to them:
You shall be holy, for I the Lord your God am holy...
When you reap a harvest, you shall not wholly reap the
corner of your field, nor shall you gather the gleaning of your
harvest. You shall not glean your vineyard, nor shall you gather
the fallen fruit of your vineyard; you shall leave them for the
poor and for the stranger...
You shall not steal; nor shall you deal falsely, nor lie to one

another. You shall not swear by My name falsely .. You shall not oppress your neighbor nor rob him. The wages of a day laborer shall not remain with you through the night. You shall not curse the deaf, nor put a stumbling-block before the blind ... You shall do no unrighteousness in judgment: being neither partial to the poor, nor favoring the mighty; but in righteousness shall you judge your neighbor. You shall not go up and down as a tale-bearer among your people; nor shall you stand idly by the blood of our neighbor ... You shall not hate your brother in your heart, but you shall surely reprimand him ... You shall not take vengeance, nor bear any grudge against the children of your people, but you shall love your neighbor as yourself.

. . . You shall stand up before the aged, and honor the face of the old man ... If a stranger sojourn with you in your land, you shall not do him wrong. The stranger who sojourns with you shall be as the homeborn among you, and you shall love him as yourself: for you too were strangers in the land of Egypt ... You shall do no unrighteousness in judgment, in yardsticks, weights, or measures. Just balances, just weights, a just ephah and a just hin shall you have. You shall observe all My statutes and all My ordinances, and do them. I am the Lord.

Leviticus 19:1-37

SABBATH

A Day of Rest For You

God blessed the seventh day, and hallowed it; because on it He rested from all His work of creation.

Genesis 2:3

Keep It Holy

Remember the sabbath day, to keep it holy. Six days shall you labor and do all your work; but the seventh day is a sabbath to the Lord your God, on it you shall not do any manner of work, you, nor your son, nor your daughter, nor your man-servant, nor your maid-servant, nor your cattle, nor your stranger who is within your gates; for in six days the Lord made heaven and earth, the sea, and all that is in them, and rested on the seventh day; wherefore the Lord blessed the sabbath day, and hallowed it.

Exodus 20:8-10

Made For Man

He said to them, the sabbath was made for man, and not man for the sabbath.

Mark 2:27

Rest for Your Field

Six years you shall sow your field, and harvest it. But the seventh year shall be a sabbath of solemn rest for the land, a sabbath to the Lord; you shall neither sow your field, nor prune your vineyard . . .

Leviticus 25:3-4

SACRIFICE

Meaningless Sacrifice

The sacrifice of a wicked person is an abomination; How much more, when he brings it with the proceeds of wickedness.

Proverbs 21:17

Offering Sacrifices

Offer the sacrifice of righteousness.

Psalms 4:6

* * *

Offer up spiritual sacrifices.

1 Peter 2:5

* * *

Let us offer the sacrifice of praise to God continually: that is, the fruit of our lips giving thanks to His name.

Hebrews 13:15

When God Tested Abraham

"Abraham, Abraham! Lay not your hand upon the boy, nor do anything to him! For now I know that you are a God-fearing man, seeing you have not withheld your son, your only beloved son, from Him."

Abraham lifted his eyes, and behind him was a ram caught in the thicket by his horns. Abraham took the ram and offered him for a sacrifice instead of his son.

Genesis 22:7-13

Sacrifice vs. Obeying God

Samuel said:
"Has the Lord as great delight in burnt-offerings and sac-
rifices,
As in hearkening to the voice of the Lord?
Behold, to obey is better than sacrifice,
And to hearken than the fat of rams."

1 Samuel 15:22

A Contrite Heart

O Lord, open my lips
And my mouth shall declare Your praise.
For You delight not in sacrifice nor in burnt-offering.
The sacrifices to God are a contrite spirit;
A humble and a contrite heart, O God,
You will not despise.

Psalms 51:17-19

Righteousness and Justice

To do righteousness and justice is more acceptable to the
Lord than sacrifice.

Proverbs 21:3

Amos Taunts Israel for Her Idolatry

"Come to Beth-El and sin! Bring your sacrifices in the morning, and your tithes after three days! Offer a thanksgiving
sacrifice of leavened bread, and proclaim your free-will offerings. For so you love to do, O children of Israel!"

Amos 4:4-5

SALVATION

The Lord is Salvation

The Lord is my strength and song,
And he has become my salvation.

Exodus 15:2

*   *   *

The Lord is my light and my salvation:

Whom shall I fear?
The Lord is the stronghold of my life;
Of whom shall I be afraid?

Psalms 27:1

* * *

Whoever shall call upon the name of the Lord shall be saved.

Romans 10:13

Salvation Through Jesus

For God so loved the world, that he gave his only begotten Son, that whoever believes in Him should not perish, but have everlasting life.

For God sent His Son into the world not to condemn the world; but that the world through him might be saved.

John 3:16-17

The Door

I am the door: by me if any man enter in, he shall be saved.

John 10:9

A Fearful Task

Work out your salvation with fear and trembling.

Philippians 2:12

SATAN

Mark Reprimands Peter

He rebuked Peter, saying, "Get you behind me, Satan: for you do not savor the things that be of God, but the things that be of men."

Mark 8:33

SELF-RIGHTEOUSNESS

Thoughts on Self-Righteousness

Though I be righteous, my own mouth shall condemn me.

Job 9:20

* * *

They say: "Stand Back! Do not come near me, for I am holier than you."

Isaiah 65:5

You are those who justify yourselves before men: but God knows your hearts.

Luke 16:15

* * *

Be not righteous overmuch: nor make yourself overwise.

Ecclesiastes 7:16

* * *

Woe to those who are wise in their own eyes, and prudent in their own sight!

Isaiah 5:21

The Angry Prophet and God's Reproof

Jonah then went a short distance from the city of Nineveh, made himself a booth and waited under it to see what would become of the city. When the Lord God made a gourd grow over Jonah's head to provide him with shade from the heat, Jonah was pleased. But next morning God produced a worm which attacked the gourd so that it withered. And as the sun rose God sent a fierce east wind and the sun beat down upon Jonah so that he felt faint and prayed for death, saying:

"It would be better for me to die than to live!"

But God said to Jonah:

"Are you really angry about the gourd?"

"So angry I could die!" he answered.

Then the Lord said:

"You are concerned about the gourd, which you never labored for and which came up in a single night and perished in a night. Should I not be concerned about Nineveh, the great city where there are more than one-hundred-and-twenty-thousand persons who cannot tell their right hand from their left, as well as many cattle?"

Jonah 4:5-11

SERVICE

How to Serve

By love serve one another.

Galatians 5:13

* * *

Whatever you do, do it heartily — for the Lord and not for me,

knowing that you shall receive your reward from the Lord.
Colossians 3:23

* * *

Be kindly affectioned one to another with brotherly love; in honor preferring one another; not slothful in business; fervent in spirit; serving the Lord.

Romans 12:10, 11

Worshiping the Lord

All nations shall come and worship before You.
Revelations 15:4

* * *

You shall worship the Lord your God, and Him only shall you serve.

Luke 4:8

* * *

I bend my knees to the Father of Our Lord Jesus Christ.
Ephesians 3:14

The Two Sisters Mary and Martha

Jesus and his disciples came to a village where 'a woman, Martha, welcomed him into her home. Her sister Mary immediately sat at Jesus' feet and listened to his words. Martha, who was busy serving, came to him and complained:

"Lord, do you not care that my sister is letting me do all the serving? Tell her to help me."

Jesus replied:

"Martha, Martha, you are concerned and busy with so many things while only one thing is needed. Mary has chosen the important thing, and it shall not be taken from her."

Luke 10:38-42

Gideon's Call to Service

Now Gideon was beating out wheat in the winepress — to hide it from the Midianites who had been destroying all the produce of the land — when the angel of the Lord appeared to him and said:

"The Lord is with you, mighty man of valor!"

Replied Gideon: "If the Lord is with us, why then has all this befallen us? Where are all His wondrous works which our fathers told us of? Now He has delivered us into the hands of the Midian!"

"Go," the angel said, and save Israel from the Midianites."

Gideon said: "Oh, my lord, how can I save Israel? My family is the poorest in Menasseh, and I am the least in my father's house."

The angel said: "The Lord will surely be with you."

Judges 6:11-16

The Call of Saul

Samuel spoke thus to Saul:

"On whom is all the desire of Israel? Is it not on you and your father's house?"

Saul replied:

"Am I not a Benjamite, the smallest of the tribes of Israel? And my family the least of the tribe of Benjamin? So why do you speak to me in this way?"

1 Samuel 9:21

Fishers of Men

Jesus, walking by the sea of Galilee, saw two brothers, Simon called Peter, and Andrew, casting a net into the sea: for they were fishermen. He said to them: "Follow me and I will make you fishers of men."

Matthew 4:18-19

Harvests for the Lord

The harvest truly is great, but the laborers are few: pray you therefore the Lord of the harvest, that He send forth laborers to His harvest.

Luke 10:2

SIN

King David Acknowledges His Sin

Nathan, the prophet, asked:

"Why have you despised the commandment of the Lord and done evil in His sight? You have killed Uriah the Hittite with the sword of the Ammonites and taken his wife."

And David said: "I have sinned against the Lord."

2 Samuel 12:9, 13

Self-Deceit

If we say that we have no sin, we deceive ourselves, and the truth is not in us.

John 1:8

The Lamb of God

Behold the Lamb of God, who takes away the sin of the world.

John 1:29

Wages of Sin

The wage of sin is death.

Romans 6:23

Who Is Without Sin?

"He who is without sin among you, let him first cast a stone at her."
And Jesus said to the woman:
"Go, and sin no more."

John 8:7, 11

The Searcher

You search after my sin.

Job 10:6

Jesus "Explains" the Company He Keeps

As Jesus sat eating in Matthew's house, many publicans and sinners came and sat down with him and his disciples . . .
Said Jesus:
"Those who are in good health do not need a physician; the sick do . . . I have not come to call the righteous to repentance, but sinners."

Matthew 9:12-13

SLAVERY

Pharaoh Enslaves the Israelites

Now there arose a new king over Egypt who knew not Joseph. He said to his people:

"See how many and mighty the children of Israel are becoming! Come, let us deal shrewdly with them lest they multiply and, if we are at war, join our enemies to fight against us and leave our land."

Therefore he set taskmasters over them to oppress them with cruel and heavy labor. And they had to build the storage cities of Pithom and Raamses for Pharaoh. He made them serve as slaves, making their lives bitter with hard work in mortar and brick in the fields.

But the more they were oppressed the more they multiplied and spread ...

Exodus 1:8-14

SONG

Singer of Israel

The saying of David, the son of Jesse ... the sweet singer of Israel.

2 Samuel 23:1

Sing to the Lord

O sing to the Lord a new song.

Psalms 96:1

In Praise of Saul and David

The women played and sang:
"Saul has slain his thousands,
And David his ten thousands."

1 Samuel

The Vineyard

Let me sing of my beloved,
A song of my beloved touching his vineyard.
My beloved had a vineyard
In a very fruitful hill;
He dug it and cleared it of stones,
And planted the choicest vine ...
He expected it to bring forth grapes,
But it brought forth wild grapes.

Now, O inhabitants of Jerusalem and men of Judah,
What more could have been done for my vineyard,

That I have not done?
Why, when I expected it to bring forth grapes,
Did it bring forth wild grapes?...
The vineyard of the Lord of hosts is the house of Israel,
And the men of Judah the plant of his delight;
He looked for justice, but behold, violence!
For righteousness, but behold a cry!

Isaiah 5:1-7

From Miriam's Song

Miriam took a timbrel in her hand; and all the women went
out after her with timbrels and with dances; and Miriam led
them in singing:
"Sing to the Lord, for He is gloriously victorious;
The horse and his rider has He thrown into the sea..."

Exodus 15:20-21

From the Song of Moses

Moses spoke the words of this song in the ears of all the
assembly of Israel:
"Give ear, O heavens, and I will speak;
And let the earth hear the words of my mouth..."

Deuteronomy 32:1

From Deborah's Song

Then sang Deborah and Barak on that day:
"Hear, O Kings; give ear, O princes;
I, to the Lord will I sing:
I will sing praise to the Lord, the God of Israel...
Awake, awake Deborah;
Awake, awake, utter a song;
Arise, Barak, and lead your oppressors captive, son of
Abinoam!"

Judges 5:3, 12

SONS

Isaac Blesses Jacob

After eating the venison and drinking the wine, Isaac said:
"Come near now and kiss me, my son." As Jacob kissed him,
Isaac smelled the fragrance of his clothes and blessed him

saying:
"The smell of my son
Is like the smell of a field that the Lord has blessed.
May God give you of the dew of heaven,
And of the fertility of the earth,
And plenty of corn and wine.
Let peoples serve you
And nations bow down to you!
Be master of your brothers
And may your mother's sons bow down to you."

Genesis 27:25-29

Isaac Blesses Esau

When Esau heard that his brother Jacob had gotten the blessing meant for *him*, Esau cried out:
"Have you only one blessing, my father? Bless me too!" And Esau wept.

Finally Isaac said:
"Far from the fertile places of the earth shall be your dwelling;
Far from the dew of the heavens;
By your sword you shall live, and you shall serve your brother . . . "

Genesis 27:38-40

Parable of the Prodigal Son

A man had two sons. The younger of them said to his father: "Father, give me the portion of goods that will fall to me." So his father divided the inheritance between them.

Soon the younger son gathered everything together and journeyed to a distant country where he wasted his substance with riotous living.

When he had spent everything, there arose a mighty famine in that land, and he began to be in want.

So he hired himself to a citizen of that country who sent him to his farm to feed the swine.

He would have liked to have filled his belly with the husks the swine ate, but nobody gave him anything.

Reflecting about this, he thought: How many hired servants of my father's have bread enough and to spare and here I am starving! I will go to my father and say: "Father, I have sinned against heaven and you, and am no longer worthy to be called your son: take me as one of your hired servants."

And he set off for his father's. But when he was still a great way off, his father saw him, and he had compassion, and ran and fell on his neck and kissed him.

"Father," the son said to him, "I have sinned against heaven and you, and am no longer worthy to be called your son."

But the father said to his servants:

"Bring out the best robe and put it on him; and put a ring on his hand and shoes on his feet. And bring here the fatted calf and kill it; and let us eat and be merry. For this my son was dead, and is alive again; he was lost and is found ... "

Luke 15:11-24

SORCERY

Saul Consults the Witch of Endor

Then Saul said to his servants:

"Find me a woman who is a medium so that I may inquire of her."

His servants answered him:

"There is a woman medium in Endor."

Saul then disguised himself, putting on other clothes and went with two of his men. They came to the woman by night and Saul said:

"Divine for me, I pray you, through a ghost, and bring up for me whomever I name."

The woman answered:

"You know how Saul has gotten rid of all mediums in the land. Why do you lay a snare for my life, to have me killed?"

But Saul swore to her:

"As the Lord lives, no punishment shall happen to you for this."

"Whom shall I bring up for you?" the woman asked.

"Samuel."

When the woman saw Samuel, she screamed:

"Why have you deceived me? You are Saul!"

"Do not be afraid," the king said. "What do you see?"

The woman answered:

"An old man, covered with a robe."

Saul knew it was Samuel and he bowed his face to the ground.

Samuel then said to Saul:

"Why do you disturb me by bringing me up?"

Saul replied:

"I am greatly distressed, for the Philistines are making war against me and God has left me. He no longer answers me through prophets or dreams, so I have called on you to tell me what I should do."

Samuel said:

"Why do you ask me, seeing that the Lord has left you and has become your enemy? The Lord has rent the kingdom from you and given it to another, to David . . . The Lord will deliver the army of Israel into the hand of the Philistines and tomorrow you and your sons will be with me."

1 Samuel 28:7-19

SPEECH

To Everything a Time

There is a time to keep silence, and a time to speak.

Ecclesiastes 3:7

Slander

Do violence to no man, neither accuse any falsely.

Luke 3:14

Tale-Bearing

You shall not go up and down as a tale-bearer among your people.

Leviticus 19:16

Control Your Tongue

Keep your tongue from evil, and your lips from speaking guile.

Psalms 34:14

* * *

Let your speech always be gracious, seasoned with salt; and know how you ought to answer any person properly.

Colossians 4:6

On Speaking Up

A word in due season, how good it is!

Proverbs 16:23

A Soft Answer

A soft answer turns away wrath; but a grievous word stirs up anger.

Proverbs 15:1

SPIRIT

God's Spirit

Then shall the dust return to the earth as it was. And the spirit return to God who gave it.

Ecclesiastes 12:7

A New Spirit

A new heart will I give you, and a new spirit will I put within you.

Ezekiel 36:26

The Willing Spirit

The spirit is willing but the flesh is weak.

Matthew 26:41

Life-Giving

Not of the letter, but of the spirit: for the letter kills, while the spirit gives life.

2 Corinthians 3:6

Body Without Spirit

Take no thought of your life, what you shall eat or drink; nor of your body, what you shall put on. Is not the life more than meat, and the body than clothes?

Matthew 6:25

* * *

The body without the spirit is dead.

James 2:26

Spiritual Blindness

Leave them alone: they are blind leading the blind. And if the blind lead the blind, both shall fall into the ditch.

Matthew 15:14

Spiritual Food and Drink

Jesus said to them, I am the bread of life: he who comes to me shall never hunger; and he who believes in me shall never thirst.

John 6:35

Unleavened Bread for the Passover

Do you not know that a little leaven leavens the whole lump? Therefore let us keep the feast of Passover not with the leaven of malice and wickedness, but with the unleavened bread of sincerity and truth.

Corinthians 5:6-8

Spiritual Values

He said to Peter:
"Get behind me, Satan! You are an offence to me, for you savor not the things of God, but those of men."

Matthew 16:23

* * *

Not what goes into the mouth defiles a man: but what comes out of the mouth.

Matthew 15:11

Spiritual Treasures

Lay not up for yourselves treasures upon earth, where moth and rust corrupt, and where thieves break through and steal. But lay up for yourselves treasures in heaven . . . For where your treasure is, there will your heart be also.

Matthew 6:19-21

Fruit of the Spirit

The works of the flesh are manifest, which are these: Adultery, fornication, uncleanness, lasciviousness . . .
But the fruit of the Spirit is love, joy, peace, patience, gentleness, goodness, faith . . . Let us not desire vain glory, provoking one another, envying one another.

Galatians 5:19-26

STRENGTH

Delilah Ferrets Out Samson's Secret

"How can you say, 'I love you,' " Delilah said, "when you do not trust me? You have mocked me three times and have not told me the secret of your strength."

And she pressed him day after day until he was wearied to death and he told her his secret.

Samson said:

"No razor has touched my head. I have been a Nazirite from birth. If I were shaved, my strength would leave me, and I should become weak, like any other man."

Once Delilah learned Samson's secret, she sent for the lords of the Philistines, saying:

"Come at once. He has told me all."

They came and brought her the money they had promised. As soon as she had put Samson to sleep she called for a man who shaved off the seven locks of Samson's head. Then she whispered:

"The Philistines are upon you, Samson!" He awoke, thinking, "I will get up as at other times and shake myself free." But he did not know that the Lord had departed from him.

The Philistines then seized him and put out his eyes; and they brought him down to Gaza, bound him with chains of brass and set him to grinding corn in the prison-house.

Judges 16:15-22

SWEARING

Do Not Swear

Do not swear, neither by heaven nor by earth, nor by any other oath: but let your yes be yes and your no, no.

James 5:12

The Name of the Lord

You shall not take the name of the Lord your God in vain.

Deuteronomy 5:11

TEMPLE

Solomon's Prayer for Acceptance of His Temple

"I have surely built You a Temple," Solomon prayed to the Lord. "A place for You to dwell in forever . . . But will God in truth dwell on the earth? Behold, heaven and the heaven of heavens cannot contain You! How much less this temple. Yet, hearken to the prayer of Your servant, O Lord my God, and of Your people Israel. Hear in heaven, Your dwelling-place: and when You hear, forgive."

1 Kings 8:12-13, 27-30

House of the Lord

For My house shall be called a house of prayer for all people.

Isaiah 56:7

* * *

I will dwell in the house of the Lord forever.

Psalms 23:6

* * *

I was glad when they said to me,
Let us go into the house of the Lord.

Psalms 122:1

The Lord's Peace

Then Gideon built an altar there to the Lord, and called it "Adonai-shalom" (the Lord is Peace).

Judges 6:24

David the Warrior Forbidden

"You shall not build a house for My name, because you are a man of war, and have shed blood."

1 Chronicles 28:3

A Demonstration at the Temple

When he and his disciples came to Jerusalem, Jesus went into the temple and began to drive out those who were selling and buying. He overturned the tables of the moneychangers and the seats of those selling doves; and he would not let anybody carry any vessels through the temple. And he began teaching:

"Is it not written, 'My house shall be called a house of prayer for all peoples'? But you have made it a den of thieves."

Mark 11:15-17

Only Righteousness Can Save

Hear the message that came to Jeremiah from the Lord, saying: Stand in the gate of the Lord's house, and proclaim:

"Mend your ways and your doings, that I may remain with you in this place. Trust not in misleading words: 'This is the Temple of the Lord! The Temple of the Lord! The Temple of the Lord!' No, only if you thoroughly mend your ways and your doings; if you thoroughly execute justice between a man and his neighbor; if you do not oppress the stranger, the fatherless, and the widow, and do not shed innocent blood in this place, nor walk after other gods to your hurt — only then will I cause you to dwell in this place, in the land that I gave to your fathers, for ever and ever.

"Will you steal, murder, and commit adultery, and swear falsely, and offer incense to Baal, and walk after strange gods and come and stand before Me in this house? Has this house, which carries My name, become a den of robbers in your eyes?"

Jeremiah 7:1-11

David Charges Solomon

David called for his son Solomon and said:

"My son, it was in my heart to build a house to the Lord my God. But the word of the Lord came to me saying: 'You have shed too much blood and waged great wars, so you may not build a house to My name ... But a son shall be born to you who shall be a man of peace. Him I will give rest from all neighboring enemies. His name shall be Solomon, and I will give peace and quietness to Israel in his days. It is he who shall build a house to My name. He shall be a son to Me and I will be a father to him, establishing the throne of his kingdom over Israel forever.'

"Now, my son, the Lord be with you. Prosper and build the house of the Lord your God as He has spoken to me. And may the Lord give you discretion and understanding in your rule over Israel to keep the law of the Lord your God. Then, if you observe the statutes and ordinances with which the Lord charged Moses, you shall prosper. Be strong and of good courage. Do not fear or be dismayed ... Get started and the Lord be with you!"

1 Chronicles 22:6-13, 16

Worshiping in God's House

How lovely are Your tabernacles,

O Lord of hosts!
My soul yearns and pines
   for the courts of the Lord.
My heart and my flesh sing for
   joy to the living God.
Yes, the sparrow has found a
   house, and the swallow a nest for herself
Where she may lay her young;
Your altars, O Lord of hosts,
My King, and my God.
For a day in Your courts is better
   than a thousand elsewhere;
I had rather be a doorkeeper in
   the house of my God,
Than dwell in the tents of wickedness.

Psalms 84:2-5, 11

TEMPTATION

Resist Temptation

Watch and pray that you do not enter into temptation: the spirit indeed is willing, but the flesh is weak.

Matthew 26:41

Deliverance

Lead us not into temptation, but deliver us from evil.

Matthew 6:13

The Blessed One

Blessed is the man who endures temptation: for once he has been tried, he will receive the crown of life, which the Lord has promised to those who love him.

James 1:12

THANKSGIVING

Thanks to the Lord

This is the day which the Lord has made; we will rejoice and be glad in it.

Psalms 118:24

*   *   *

Let us offer the sacrifice of praise to God continually; that is, the fruit of our lips giving thanks to His name.

Hebrews 13:15

* * *

O give thanks to the Lord, for He is good, for His mercy endures forever.

Psalms 107:1

* * *

Open to me the gates of righteousness: I will enter them and I will give thanks to the Lord.

Psalms 118:19

* * *

It is a good thing to give thanks to the Lord!

Psalms 92:2

A Psalm of Thanksgiving

Shout joyfully to the Lord, all you lands;
Serve the Lord with gladness;
Come before His presence with singing.
Know that the Lord is God;
It is He Who has made us, and we are His,
His people, and the flock of His pasture.
Enter into His gates with thanksgiving,
And into His courts with praise;
Give thanks to Him, and bless His name.
For the Lord is good; His mercy endures forever;
and His faithfulness, to all generations.

Psalms 100

With God's Help

When you have eaten and are satisfied, and have built goodly houses, and lived in them; and when your herds and flocks multiply . . . and all that you have is multiplied and your heart is lifted up, do not forget the Lord your God, who brought you out of the house of bondage . . . and say: "My power and the might of my own hand have gotten me this wealth!" Remember, it is the Lord your God who gives you power to get this wealth.

Deuteronomy 8:12-18

TIME

A Season For Everything

To every thing there is a season, and a time to every purpose
   under the heaven:
A time to be born, and a time to die;
A time to plant, and a time to pluck up that which is planted;
A time to kill, and a time to heal;
A time to break down, and a time to build up;
A time to weep, and a time to laugh;
A time to mourn, and a time to dance;
A time to cast away stones, and a time to gather stones to-
   gether;
A time to embrace, and a time to refrain from embracing;
A time to seek, and a time to lose;
A time to keep, and a time to cast away;
A time to rend, and a time to sew;
A time to keep silence, and a time to speak;
A time to love, and a time to hate;
A time for war, and a time for peace.

Ecclesiastes 3:1-8

Time in God's Sight

A thousand years in Your sight
Are but as yesterday when it is past
And as a watch in the night.

Psalms 90:4

* * *

One day from the Lord's view is as a thousand years, and a
thousand years are as one day.

2 Peter 3:8

Time Overtakes to All

I saw that the race is not to the swift, nor the battle to the
strong, neither yet bread to the wise, nor yet riches to men of
understanding, nor yet favor to men of skill; but time and
chance happens to them all.

Ecclesiastes 9:11

TRUST

Trust Not in Man

Put not your trust in princes,

Nor in the son of man.

Psalms 146:3

Not in Worldly Wealth

Charge the rich not to trust in worldly riches but in the living God, who gives us richly all things to enjoy.

1 Timothy 6:17

Refuge in the Lord

Out of my straits I called upon the Lord;
The Lord answered me and set me free . . .
It is better to take refuge in the Lord
Than to trust in princes.

Psalms 118:5, 9

Job Trusts . . . But Still Argues

As for me, I know that my Redeemer lives.

Job 19:25

* * *

Though He slay me, yet will I trust in Him;
But I will argue my ways before Him.

Job 13:15

A Psalm of Trust

The Lord is my light and my salvation;
  whom shall I fear?
The Lord is the stronghold of my life;
  of whom shall I be afraid? . . .
Though an army should encamp against me,
My heart shall not fear;
Though war should rise up against me,
Even then will I be confident . . .

Psalms 27:1-3

TRUTH

I Am the Way

I am the way, the truth, and the life: no man comes to the Father but through me.

John 14:6

Truth Leads to Freedom

You shall know the truth and the truth shall make you free . . . but whoever commits sin becomes the slave of sin.

John 8:32, 34

A Father's Joy

I have no greater joy than to hear that my children walk in truth.

3 John 4

Speak the Truth

These, then, are the things you should do:
Speak the truth to one another: render judgments of honesty and peace in your gates. Let none of you devise evil in your hearts against one another, nor love a false oath; for all these are things that I hate, says the Lord.

Zechariah 8:16-17

* * *

Lying lips are an abomination to the Lord:
But they that deal truthfully are His delight.

Proverbs 12:22

UNDERSTANDING

Childish Understanding

When I was a child, I spoke like a child, I understood like a child: but when I became a man, I put away childish things.

1 Corinthians 13:11

Through a Glass Darkly

Now we see through a glass darkly; but then we shall see face to face: now I know things only in part; but then I shall know them even as God knows me now.

1 Corinthians 13:12

UNITY

Divisiveness

If a house is divided against itself, that kingdom cannot stand.

Mark 3:25

VANITY

Striving After Wind

The words of Koheleth (the Preacher),
the son of David, king of Jerusalem.
Vanity of vanities, says the Preacher,
Vanity of vanities, all is vanity.
What profit has man of all his labor
In which he labors under the sun?
One generation passes away, and another generation
    emerges;
And the earth abides forever.
The sun also rises, and the sun goes down,
And hastens to its place where it rose.
The wind goes toward the south
And turns about to the north;
It whirls about continually,
And the wind returns again to its circuits.
All the rivers run into the sea,
Yet the sea is not full;
To the place where the rivers go,
There they go again.
The eye is not satisfied with seeing,
Nor the ear filled with hearing.
What has been is what shall be,
What has been done is what shall be done.
There is nothing new under the sun.
I have seen all the works that are done under the sun:
All is vanity and a striving after wind.

                                    Ecclesiastes: 1:9-14

VENGEANCE

Take Not Vengeance

You shall not take vengeance, nor bear any grudge against
the children of your people, but you shall love your neighbor as
yourself.

                                    Leviticus 19:18

*   *   *

Vengeance is Mine.

                                    Deuteronomy 32:35

Avenge not yourselves, but rather give place to God's wrath: for it is written, "Vengeance is Mine; I will repay, says the Lord. Therefore, if your enemy is hungry, feed him; if he is thirsty, give him drink . . . "

Romans 12:19-20

WAR

A Response to Violence

Whoever shall strike you on your right cheek, turn to him the other also.

Matthew 5:39

* * *

Then Jesus said to him: "Put back your sword: for all those who take the sword shall perish by the sword."

Matthew 26:52

Saul and David

Saul hath slain his thousands, and David his ten thousands.

Samuel 18:7

Vengeance Repaid

Vengeance is mine: I will repay, saith the Lord.

Romans 12:19

Weapons of War

How are the mighty fallen; and the weapons of war perished!

2 Samuel 1:27

A Time for Everything

There is a time to kill, and a time to heal . . . A time for war, and a time for peace.

Ecclesiastes 3:3, 8

Defending Your Own Land

When you go to war in your own land against an adversary that attacks you, then you shall sound an alarm with your trumpets; and you shall be remembered before the Lord your God, and you shall be saved from your enemies.

Numbers 10:9

Scattered Peoples

God has scattered the peoples who delight in war!

Psalms 68:31

Preparation in Self-Defense

Proclaim this among the nations,
Prepare war,
Stir up the mighty men!
Let all the men of war draw near,
Let them come up.
Beat your plowshares into swords,
And your pruning-hooks into spears;
Let the weak say: "I am strong."
Hurry, and come, all neighboring nations,
And gather yourselves together.
There cause Your mighty ones to come down, O Lord!

Joel 4:9-11

Goliath's Challenge

And there went out a champion from the camp of the Philistines named Goliath. His height was six cubits. He had a helmet of brass, he was clad with a coat of mail, and the weight of his coat was five thousand shekels of brass . . .

He cried out to the armies of Israel:

"Why are you set up in battle array? Am I not a Philistine and you the servants of Saul? Choose a man from among you and let him come down to me. If he be able to fight me and kill me then we will be your servants; but if I prevail and kill him, then you shall be our servants. I defy the armies of Israel! Give me a man to fight."

When Saul and the Israelites heard those words of the Philistine, they were greatly afraid.

Samuel 17:4-11

Exemption From Military Service

When a man takes a new wife, he need not go out in the army, nor shall he be charged with any public business; he shall be free for his household for one year, to cheer his wife whom he has taken.

Deuteronomy 24:5

Cleanliness in Camp

You shall have a place also outside the camp, where you shall go. And you shall have a paddle among your weapons; and when you sit down there, you shall dig with it, and shall cover that which comes from you. For the Lord your God walks in the midst of your camp, to deliver you, and to give up your enemies before you; therefore shall your camp be holy; that He see no unseemly thing in you, and turn away from you.

Deuteronomy 23:13-15

Do Not Destroy Fruit Trees

When you besiege a city . . . you shall not destroy its trees; for is the tree of the field like man that it should be besieged? Only the trees which you know are not trees for food, may you cut to build bulwarks against the city that is at war with you.

Deuteronomy 20:19-20

Release from Army Service

The officers shall speak to the people saying:

"Who has built a new house and has not dedicated it? Let him go and return to his house, lest he die in the battle, and another man dedicate it. Who has planted a vineyard and has not enjoyed its fruit? Let him go and return to his house, lest he die in the battle, and another man enjoy the fruit. Who has betrothed a wife, and has not taken her for his wife? Let him go and return to his house, lest he die in the battle, and another man take her for his wife.

The officers shall speak further to the people and say:

"What man is there who is fearful and faint-hearted? Let him go and return to his house, lest he make his brethren faint-hearted like himself."

Deuteronomy 20:5-7

Treatment of a Woman Captive

When the Lord your God delivers your enemies into your hands, and you carry them away captive and see among them a woman of goodly form whom you have a desire for and want her as your wife, you shall bring her home to your house. But first she must shave her head, pare her nails, and lay aside the garb of her captivity. She shall remain in your house and mourn her father and her mother a full month before you may go in to her, and be her husband, and she be your wife. Later, if you have no delight in her, then you shall let her have her freedom, if she wants; but you shall not sell her or make her a slave, since you had forced her to marry you.

Deuteronomy 21:10-14

WEALTH

On Worldly Goods

For when the rich man dies he shall carry nothing away;
His glory shall not descend after him.

Psalms 49:17-18

* * *

Naked I came out of my mother's womb,
And naked I shall return:
The Lord gave, and the Lord has taken away;
Blessed be the name of the Lord.

Job 1:21

* * *

We brought nothing into this world, and it is certain we can carry nothing out.

1 Timothy 6:7

* * *

The love of money is the root of all evil.

1 Timothy 6:10

* * *

Teaching things which they ought not, for filthy lucre's sake.

Titus: 11

The Rich Living High

Woe to them that are at ease in Zion,
And to those who think themselves secure in the mountain of
  Samaria!
The nobles and leaders of the nation who lie upon beds of
  ivory,

Stretch themselves upon their couches,
Eat the lambs out of the flock,
And the calves out of the midst of the stall;
Who thrum on the psaltery,
Devise instruments of music, like David;
Drink wine by the bowl,
Anoint themselves with the best ointments —
But have no care for the afflictions of the nation.

Amos 6:1-6

A Heap of Riches

He heapeth up riches, and knoweth not who shall gather them.

Psalms 39:6

Depending on Money

He that trusteth in his riches shall fall.

Proverbs 11:14

Getting to Heaven

It is easier for a camel to go through the eye of a needle, than for a rich man to enter into the kingdom of God.

Matthew 10:24

Merchants Cheating the Poor

Hear this, O you who would swallow the needy,
And destroy the poor of the land,
Saying: "When will the new moon be gone, that we may sell grain?
And the Sabbath, that we may set forth corn?
We will make the ephah small, and the shekel great,
And falsify the scales;
We will buy the poor for silver,
And the needy for a pair of shoes,
And sell even the refuse of the corn."

Amos 8:4-6

Wine Maketh Merry

A feast is made for laughter, and wine maketh life merry; but money answereth all things.

Ecclesiastes 10:19

Worldly vs. Spiritual Wealth

For what does it profit a man if he gains the whole world and loses his own soul?

Matthew 16:26

Denouncing the Extravagant and Callous

Hear this, you cows of Bashan,
Women on the mountain of Samaria
Who oppress the poor, crush the needy,
And say to your lords,
   "Bring, that we may feast."
Lo, the day shall come
When you shall be taken away with hooks,
Every last one of you with fish-hooks,
Through the breaches of the walls.

Amos 4:1-3

WISDOM

The Beginning

The beginning of wisdom is: get wisdom;
Yes, with all your getting, get understanding.
Extol her, and she will exalt you;
She will bring you honor, when you embrace her.
She will give you a crown of grace and of glory.

Proverbs 4:7-9

Making Every Day Count

So teach us to number our days, that we may apply our hearts unto wisdom.

Psalms 90:12

The Source of Wisdom

The fear of the Lord is the beginning of knowledge;
But the foolish despise wisdom and discipline.

Proverbs 1:7

The Joys of Wisdom

Happy is the man who finds wisdom,
And the man who obtains understanding.
For the merchandise of it is better than the merchandise of

silver,
And the gain thereof, than fine gold.
She is more precious than rubies;
And all the things you can desire are not to be compared to her.

Proverbs 3:13-15

A Tree of Life

Her ways are ways of pleasantness,
And all her paths are peace.
She is a tree of life to those that lay hold upon her,
And happy is everyone who holds her fast.

Proverbs 3:14-18

Value of Wisdom

Wisdom is better than rubies.

Proverbs 8:11

The Cry of Wisdom

Wisdom crieth without; she uttereth her voice in the streets.

Proverbs 1:20

Wisdom and Knowledge

In much wisdom is much grief: and he that increaseth knowledge increaseth sorrow.

Ecclesiastes 1:2

The End of Wisdom

No doubt, you are the people, and wisdom shall die with you.

Job 12:2

A Wise Heart

A wise and an understanding heart.

I Kings 3:12

Wisdom and Grief

In much wisdom is much grief: and he who increases knowledge increases sorrow.

Ecclesiastes 1:18

Misapplied Wisdom

They are wise to do evil, but to do good they have no knowledge.

Jeremiah 4:22

Where Is Wisdom?

But where shall wisdom be found?
And where is the place of understanding? The depth says, "It is not in me."
And the sea says, "It is not with me." It cannot be gotten for It cannot be gotten for gold.
Neither can silver be weighed for its price.

Job 28:12, 14, 15

Solomon's Wish

The Lord appeared to Solomon in a dream and said: "Ask what I shall give you."

Solomon answered: "You have made me king in the place of David my father. But I am a youth who does not know how to rule. Give your servant, therefore, an understanding heart to judge, so that I may know between right and wrong in dealing with this great and multitudinous people."

The speech pleased the Lord, and God said:

"Because you have not asked long life for yourself, nor riches, nor the life of your enemies, but only for understanding, lo, I have given you a wise and understanding heart, and riches and honor as well."

1 Kings 3:5-13

The Wisdom of Solomon

God gave Solomon wisdom and understanding and largeness of heart like the sand on the seashore. Solomon's wisdom was greater than the wisdom of all the peoples of the East, and all the wisdom of Egypt. He was wiser than all men; and his fame was everywhere. He made up three thousand proverbs and his songs were a thousand and five. He knew about trees, from the cedar that is in Lebanon to the hyssop that springs out of the wall; and about beasts, birds, reptiles and fishes. And people came from kingdoms all over the world to hear the wisdom of Solomon.

1 Kings 5:9-14

King Solomon and the Two Mothers

Two women came before the king.

One woman said:

"Oh, my lord, I and this woman dwell in one house; and I gave birth to a child. Three days later this woman also gave birth. We were alone together; there was no one else in the house. Now this woman's child died during the night because she lay upon it. She arose at midnight, and took my son from me, while I slept, and laid it in her bosom, then laid her dead child in my bosom. When I rose in the morning to nurse my child, behold, it was dead. But when I looked more closely at it in the morning, I saw that it was not my son!"

The other woman said:

"No. The living child is my son, and the dead child is yours."

"No, the dead child is yours and the living child is mine!" Thus they spoke before the king.

Said King Solomon: "Fetch me a sword." And he said: "Divide the living child in two, and give half to one woman and half to the other."

Then the woman who was the mother of the living child cried out to the king, for she loved the child with all her heart:

"Oh, my lord, give her the living child! In no way kill it!"

But the other said:

"Divide it — and it shall be neither mine nor yours."

Then king Solomon said: "Give her the living child, and in no way hurt it. She is the mother."

And all Israel heard of the judgment which the king had made, and they respected him; for they saw that the wisdom of God was in him to do justice.

1 Kings 3:16-28

Virgins and Heaven

Then shall the kingdom of heaven be likened unto ten virgins which took their lamps and went forth to meet the bridegroom. And five of them were wise, and five were foolish.

Matthew 25:1-2

WOMEN

The Virtuous Woman

A woman of valor who can find?
For her price is far above rubies...
She gives food to her household,
And a portion to her maidens.
She stretches out her hand to the poor;
Yes, she reaches forth her hands to the needy.
Strength and dignity are her clothing;
And she laughs at the time to come.
She opens her mouth with wisdom;
And the law of kindness is on her tongue.
She looks well to the ways of her household,
And eats not the bread of idleness.
Her children rise up, and call her blessed;
Her husband also, and he praises her:
"Many daughters have done valiantly,
But you excell them all."
Grace is deceitful, and beauty is vain;
But a woman who reveres the Lord, she shall be praised.

Proverbs 31:10-31

Solomon's Wives

And he had seven hundred wives, princesses, and three hundred concubines: and his wives turned away his heart.

I Kings 11:3

Brevity of Life

Man, born of a woman, is short lived, and full of trouble.

Job 14:1

Women Demand Equal Rights

Then the daughters of Zelophehad drew near Moses and all the congregation, saying:

"Our father died in the wilderness and he had no sons. Why should the name of our father be taken away from his family just because he had no son? Give us a possession among our brothers."

Said the Lord to Moses:

"The daughters of Zelophehad speak right. If a man dies and

has no son, then you shall let his inheritance pass on to his daughter.''

WORDS

In the Beginning

In the beginning was the Word, and the Word was with God, and the Word was God.

John 1:1

Prayerful Words

Let the words of my mouth, and the meditation of my heart, be acceptable in thy sight.

Psalms 19:14

Using Words Wisely

Out of thine own mouth will I judge thee.

Luke 19:22

* * *

A time to be silent, and a time to speak.

Ecclesiastes 3:7

* * *

Words of truth and soberness.

Acts 26:25

* * *

A word spoken at the proper time—how good it is!

Proverbs 15:23

The Written Word

Oh that my words were now written! Oh that they were printed in a book!

Job 19:23

Words of Wisdom

Man shall not live by bread alone, but by every word that proceedeth out of the mouth of God.

Matthew 4:4

* *

A word aptly spoken is like apples of gold in settings of silver.

Proverbs 25:11

* * *

We took sweet counsel together.

Psalms 55:14

*   *   *

Thy word is a lamp unto my feet, and a light unto my path.

Psalms 119:105

*   *   *

How forcible are right words!

Job 6:25

Smooth Talk

The words of his mouth were smoother than butter, but war was in his heart. His words were softer than oil, yet they were drawn swords.

WORKS

The Reward

Alexander the coppersmith did me much evil; the Lord reward him according to his works.

2 Timothy 4:14

*   *   *

Faith without works is dead.

James 2:26

WORLD

We Can Overcome

Be of good cheer; I have overcome the world.

John 16:33

*   *   *

Unspotted from the world.

James 1:27

Wise Children

The children of this world are in their generation wiser than the children of light.

Luke 16:8

What does a man profit if he shall gain the whole world, and lose his own soul?

Matthew 16:26

WORRY

To What End?

Which of you by taking thought can add one cubit to his stature?

Matthew 6:27

Live in the Moment

Take no thought for the morrow: for the morrow shall take thought for the things of itself. Sufficient to the day is the evil thereof.

Matthew 6:34

WORSHIP

Beauty of Holiness

Worsip the Lord in the beauty of holiness.

Psalms 29:2

WRATH

Wrath and Envy

Wrath killeth the foolish man, and envy slayeth the silly one.

Job 5:2

YEARS

Fleeting Time

A thousand years in thy sight are but as yesterday when it is past, and as a watch in the night.

Psalms 90:4

*   *   *

We bring our years to an end as a tale that is told.

Psalms 90:9

*   *   *

The days of our years are threescore years and ten; and if by reason of strength they be fourscore years, yet it is travail and vanity, for it is soon cut off, and we fly away.

Psalms 90:10

*   *   *

Jacob served seven years for Rachel; and they seemed unto him but a few days, because of the love he had for her.

Genesis 19:20

YOUTH

Rejoice in Youth

Rejoice, O young man, in thy youth. And let thy heart cheer thee in the days of thy youth.

Ecclesiastes 11:9

Strength of Youth

The glory of young men is their strength: and the beauty of old men is the hoary head.

Proverbs 20:29

Evil from Youth

The inclination of man's heart is evil from his youth.

Genesis 8:21

ZION

The Exiled Israelites Yearn for Zion

By the rivers of Babylon,
There we sat down, yes, we wept
When we remembered Zion.
Upon the willows we hung our harps.
For there our captives asked of us the words of our songs,
And our tormentors asked of us mirth, saying:
"Sing us one of your songs of Zion."
How shall we sing the Lord's song
In a foreign land?
If I forget you, O Jerusalem,
May my right hand forget its use.
May my tongue cleave to the roof of my mouth,
If I remember you not;
If I do not set Jerusalem
Above my chief joy.

Psalms 137:1-6

Isaiah Encourages the Exiles

Awake, awake,
Put on your strength, O Zion!
Put on your beautiful garments,
O Jerusalem, holy city...
Shake yourself from the dust,
Arise, and sit down, O Jerusalem,
Loose yourself from the bonds of your neck,
O captive daughter of Zion.

Isaiah 52:1-2

Redemption of the Exiles

How beautiful upon the mountains
Are the feet of the messenger of good tidings
Who announces peace, the harbinger of good tidings,
Who announces salvation;
Who says to Zion:
"Your God reigns!"
Break forth into joy, sing together,
Your waste places of Jerusalem;
For the Lord has comforted His people,
He has redeemed Jerusalem.

Isaiah 52:7-9

Prayer for the Exiles

When the Lord brought back those who returned to Zion,
We were like those who dream.
Then was our mouth filled with laughter,
And our tongue with singing.
Then said they among the nations:
"The Lord has done great things for them."
The Lord has done great things for us;
And we rejoice.
Bring back the rest of our captives, O Lord,
Like the streams in the dry land.
They who sow in tears
Shall reap in joy.

Though he goes on his way weeping who bears the measure of
  seed,
He shall come home with joy, bearing his sheaves.

Psalms 126